Are you *really* ready for college?

A College Dean's 12 Secrets for Success — what high school students don't know

Be one of the few college students to actually graduate on time!

A Guidebook for Students

(as well as parents, counselors, teachers, advisers, and others in education)

ISBN: 978-160844-320-8

Editing: Jude Neuman
Design & Layout: Michelle De Vorse
Illustration: Tom Neuman, Michelle De Vorse, Jean Christianson

for Jude

Table of Contents

A note for you —

You'll notice that this book comes to you with the important points already highlighted.

That's so you can read each chapter and then go back over the highlighted sections to review the chapter's major points. The highlights will keep these points fresh in your mind.

Because you'll use this book as a guide all through high school, you'll be returning to it many times. The highlights will help remind you of what to do to stay on track — and the reasons that staying on track is important to your future.

Why you need this book
(Who wants to be a millionaire?)

College can change your life — in many ways. For example, did you know that if you were a college graduate right now, you would earn at least $1 million more in your lifetime than a person with only a high school diploma? And if you continued in school after college, adding a professional or graduate degree, that number would double or triple. But the rewards of college are more than just financial. Research shows that people with college educations tend to have fewer problems in all areas of life, from personal relationships to health.

For these reasons and many others, more than 14 million students are enrolled in our nation's more than 4,000 two- and four-year colleges and universities. College is a big deal. As a student looking forward to higher education, you have some tremendous opportunities in your educational future. Your job as a student — and it's a big one — is to recognize and seize as many of those opportunities as you can.

Remember, however, college will be exciting and rewarding, but also demanding. You have to be prepared to face the challenges of higher education. During high school, your academic and personal maturity must grow each year, so when the time comes, you can take that giant step to college. Going to college will not be at all like going to high school. It's not just "more of the same."

The bad news

Unfortunately, far too many college students enroll as freshmen believing they are academically ready when, in fact, they are not. How do I know this? Experts who study college students paint a very grim picture. Imagine the most recent class of more than 2 million freshmen at four-year colleges. One out of four (25%) does not return to college for sophomore year — they either look for an "easier" college or they don't return to college at all. Yet their grades were good in high school, and their standardized test scores were high.

And for students attending two-year colleges, the situation is even worse. Drop-out rates are higher, and graduation rates are low.

How can that be?

Then the picture gets worse. Let's look at the numbers for four-year colleges. Only one-third of freshmen will finish in four years. Give students six years to finish, and that number will rise to only 62%. Far too many college students don't graduate *at all*. And among those who do graduate, a large number manage just to scrape by, graduating with low grades. When students take longer to graduate, it costs huge amounts of money. Students and families suffer.

What's the problem? The majority of students are not prepared to manage college studies.

Now you may say to yourself: *"My grades are good. I'll be among the one-third that makes it."* That's what most students say. The sad truth is that very good students — even excellent students — don't make it. Why? There's more involved in college success than your ACT/SAT scores and your high school grade point average. Success has to do with different kinds of abilities: your ability to manage your courses, your time, and yourself — as well as any problems that "life" presents along the way. I know this first-hand because I counseled college students for more than 25 years.

The good news

If you want to be among those who succeed, this book can show you how. **Are you *really* ready for college?** grew out of my work at a university of 7,000 undergraduates, where I was an Associate Dean for Student Academic Advising. Over the years, I advised thousands of students, and I gradually discovered that their academic problems grew out of a common set of shortcomings and inabilities.

This book shares with you 12 Strategies that I truly believe college students need to succeed. The Strategies all work together, like interlocking pieces, and form a system that will help you avoid becoming an unfortunate statistic.

The time to start using the system is now! You need to practice these Strategies while you're still in high school. Whether you know it or not, the minute you entered high school, you began to get ready for college. How you handle your high school years will determine your success in college. By applying the 12 Strategies to your high school courses, you'll be gaining valuable skills, preparing yourself for the more difficult college courses that await you.

And college is much harder. The single biggest mistake that students make is to think that college is going to be like high school, only away from home. It's not. It's very different. Unfortunately, most students don't realize this until they get to college. Then many find themselves struggling academically for the very first time. Remember all those freshmen who don't return sophomore year? They're intelligent — a great many of them just didn't know how to handle themselves. College demands planning, focus, hard work (study), and knowing how to manage yourself and your time.

Here are some basic differences between college and high school.

- Classes meet only a few times a week.
- College semesters are shorter.
- Professors pack much more content in a single semester.
- The pace of college courses is much faster than high school.
- You're responsible for knowing assigned material in a course even when it's not discussed in class.
- As a student, you're expected to study 2-3 hours for every hour you spend in the classroom.
- As a college student, learning and keeping up with courses rests entirely in your hands.

The solution

Are you *really* ready for college? shows you how to prepare to handle these responsibilities by becoming an active, confident, and productive student in high school. The book maps out how you can succeed in all of your courses — regardless of their difficulty.

Are you *really* ready for college? explains *how to manage your life — both in school and after school.* If you can understand these concepts, you will be ready for college.

What do I mean by *ready?* Think of it this way: No athlete preparing for a demanding season would play without intense practice or coaching. Neither should you go off to college without just as much practice and coaching. Students who have followed the 12-Strategy system in **Are you *really* ready for college?** find they finish with a "winning season." Plus, they are happier and less stressed while they're at it.

You'll like the way it feels to be able to manage your life. And with confidence as high as your grades, you will become more and more successful — not just for the next semester or year of school — but in the next crucial stage of your life and your education: college!

Read this guidebook and use its Strategies. You'll have better control of your education, your daily life, and your future. It'll be a great feeling.

Robert R. Neuman, Ph.D.
"Dr. Bob"

Fast facts you should know

Unprepared in coursework

According to ACT, of the 1.2 million high schoolers who took the ACT in 2003-2004, **only 22% were ready for college-level courses** in English, mathematics, and science. The ACT says *"We've made virtually no progress in the last 10 years helping them to become ready. And from everything we've seen, it's not going to get better any time soon."*

– Crisis at the Core; Preparing Students for College and Work, the American College Testing service.

Professors agree

- 84% of college faculty describe high school graduates as either **unprepared** or only **somewhat prepared** to pursue a college degree. Among the 84%, nearly one-fourth flatly state that students are **not prepared.**

- More than **40% of students** arrive on college campuses needing remedial work.

– School & College, The Chronicle of Higher Education, March 2006.

25% of freshmen drop out

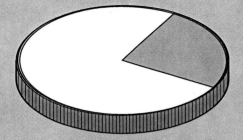

After their first year of college, **25% of** students in a freshmen class **drop out altogether or change schools to find an "easier" college.**

– A Matter of Degrees: Improving Graduation Rates in Four-Year Colleges and Universities, the Education Trust, 2004.

How long students take to graduate from college

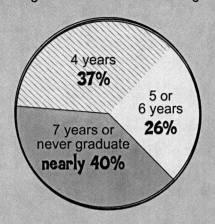

4 years
37%

5 or 6 years
26%

7 years or never graduate
nearly 40%

A Matter of Degrees: Improving Graduation Rates in Four-Year Colleges and Universities, the Education Trust, 2004.

Study time in high school

American Freshman: National Norms for Fall 2004* found that 65.6% of college-bound high school seniors studied, at most, five hours per week.

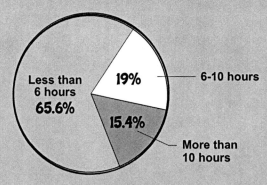

Less than 6 hours **65.6%**

19% 6-10 hours

15.4% More than 10 hours

*The American Freshman: National Norms for Fall 2004, American Council on Education, Published by the American Council on Education and University of California at Los Angeles Higher Education Research Institute.

How teens use their free time each day

Teens often "multi-task" with media, so these numbers are not necessarily separate; they often overlap. Spending little time on study leaves students ill-prepared for college.

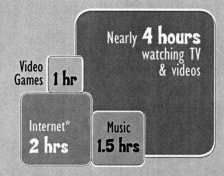

Nearly **4 hours** watching TV & videos

Video Games **1 hr**

Internet* **2 hrs**

Music **1.5 hrs**

– "Media Multi-tasking" Changing the Amount and Nature of Young People's Media Use, Kaiser Family Foundation, March 9, 2005.

* Among 10% of Internet-using students, the time spent can be considered "dependence," as with gambling, alcohol, and other addictions.

Study time in college

College professors expect students to spend at least two hours outside of class for every hour they spend in class, which equals at least **25-30 hours a weeks** for a typical course load. Consider these study times for freshmen at four-year colleges. **Only 12% of freshmen reported spending 26 or more hours a week studying.**

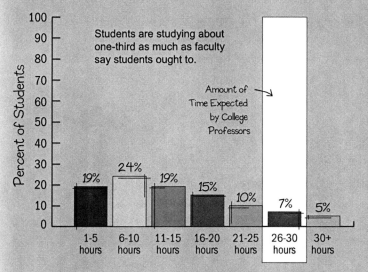

Students are studying about one-third as much as faculty say students ought to.

Amount of Time Expected by College Professors

Percent of Students

1-5 hours	6-10 hours	11-15 hours	16-20 hours	21-25 hours	26-30 hours	30+ hours
19%	24%	19%	15%	10%	7%	5%

– Jeffrey R. Young, Homework? What Homework?, The Chronicle of Higher Education, December 6, 2002.

The top 10 reasons that students leave or drop out of college

1. Too much fun and not enough study
2. Homesickness and feeling isolated
3. Academically unprepared
4. Financial constraints
5. Personal family issues
6. Academic climate
7. Lack of advising or guidance
8. Chose wrong area of study
9. Demands of a part-time job
10. Move to a different geographic location

Are you *really* ready for college? addresses 9 of these issues.

High school grades of college-bound students

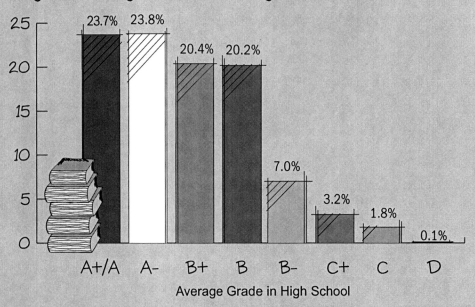

Average Grade in High School

23.7% (A+/A), 23.8% (A-), 20.4% (B+), 20.2% (B), 7.0% (B-), 3.2% (C+), 1.8% (C), 0.1% (D)

– *The American Freshman: National Norms for Fall 2004,* American Council on Education, Published by the American Council on Education and University of California at Los Angeles Higher Education Research Institute.

High school grades : a comparison

A comparison of the grades that college-bound high schotolers earned in the 1960s with the grades today's students earn.

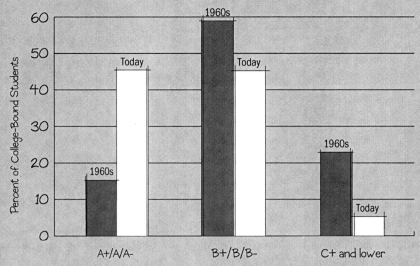

Percent of College-Bound Students

A+/A/A-, B+/B/B-, C+ and lower

– *The American Freshman: National Norms for Fall 2004,* American Council on Education, Published by the American Council on Education and University of California at Los Angeles Higher Education Research Institute.

Dangerous ideas many high school students accept as true

- Meeting high school graduation requirements will prepare me for college.
- Getting into college is the hardest part.
- It's better to take easier classes in high school and get better grades.
- My senior year in high school doesn't matter.
- I don't have to worry about grades or what classes I take until my sophomore year.
- I can take whatever classes I want when I get to college.

– An excerpt from *Betraying the College Dream*, Andrea Venezia, Michael W. Kirst, and Anthony L. Antonio, The Bridge Project Headquartered at the Stanford Institute for Higher Education Research, http://siher.stanford.edu, March, 2003.

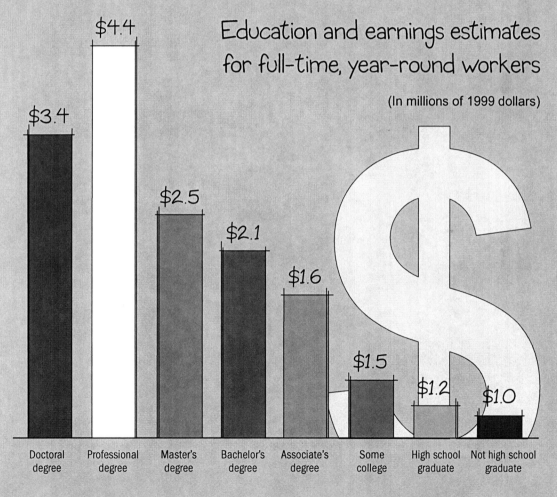

Education and earnings estimates for full-time, year-round workers

(In millions of 1999 dollars)

Doctoral degree	Professional degree	Master's degree	Bachelor's degree	Associate's degree	Some college	High school graduate	Not high school graduate
$3.4	$4.4	$2.5	$2.1	$1.6	$1.5	$1.2	$1.0

These numbers are based on the most recent census.

– *The Big Payoff: Education Attainment and Synthetic Estimates of Work-Life Earnings*, U.S. Census Bureau, Special Studies, July, 2002.

How to think about your education
(Put on your climbing boots.)

*There are lots of ways to think of your education. You could say it's like taking a journey or laying a foundation for a building. Personally, I like to think of it as climbing a mountain — it's an adventure, and it's challenging. Getting to the top requires intelligence, dedication, training, guidance, stamina, and a strong sense of purpose. To get to the top, you have to **want** to get there.*

You began your journey up the educational mountain when you were very young. For the first part of your climb (preschool, kindergarten, and grade school), the terrain was pretty easy. Your teachers helped you take each step. Your parents held your hand to keep you from tripping and falling or losing your way. The lower part of the mountain was more like walking in the woods.

Then you reached a plateau on your climb when you began middle school, and your education began to change dramatically. As you worked your way through middle school, the slope began to rise more steeply above you. The incline grew too sharp for just walking. Instead, you found yourself climbing, using your hands to pull as well as your legs to push. You were learning what other students had learned before you: Making progress in middle school takes more individual effort. From this point on, the educational mountain becomes steeper and more rugged with every passing year. More strength and courage, more careful planning and communication are required.

Now that you're in high school, the mountain's terrain has changed again: You are climbing rock face and using equipment. Your guides — teachers, counselors, parents — are still with you, but now instead of leading you, they are roped to you like a climbing team. You're doing most of the work. You are the one grappling with the rock, creating your own footholds, looking for crevices to grip, driving your spikes into the rock wall.

You communicate with your guides when you don't know how to move upward. If you can't figure out how to attack a particular part of your climb, you ask, *"What do I do now?"* Or, if you start to slip, you need to ask, *"How do I regain my footing?"* Asking the right questions, using your strength, and keeping yourself sharp and organized will get you through the tough places.

During the high school stage on the mountain, you have more personal responsibility than ever. At this elevation, you're expected to be fairly independent — for example, to know where you are going and where you are in relation to others on your rope. To check your equipment at each level of ascent. To pay attention to the weather, looking for signs of oncoming storms. You have to think on your own and keep your eye on the summit. You only get one chance on this mountain!

The higher you go up the mountain (the harder the courses), the more climbing skills you will need — along with mental and physical strength, stamina, and intelligence.

Sometimes you'll be able to see the summit clearly. Other times it will be hidden in clouds. When you lose sight of the summit, it's time to talk to a guide. You don't want to get lost or take a longer or more dangerous route than is needed. The end of high school marks the last plateau before the summit. To reach the summit, you must finish college, and from there you'll look out over a vista that's the rest of your life: more education or a career. It's your future. It should be breathtaking. It's the new world on the other side. And it's yours to explore. Why? Because you've worked hard to get there.

PSST! Go back over the highlighted words in this section. If you skim them, you'll get a quick review of —

- how school changes as you move up the mountain, and
- how you must adapt to the mountain as you climb.

Academic Fortunes

Your future in the Information Age
(Boot-up your mind.)

Face it. You're in for a lifetime of learning. That's what living in the Information Age, loaded with technology, will mean to you and your friends. You're already using computers to access and transfer information. In the future, the amount of information will continue to multiply enormously with every passing year. To keep whatever job you have, you'll have to continually learn to digest more and new information, then learn to apply or process it with technology that's constantly changing.

You won't have your parents' life

Education did not necessarily get your parents their jobs. Often, an employer was willing to "train" them for a job. However, your generation cannot be trained for jobs that don't even exist yet. Your working world will be nothing like your parents' world. The experts say you'll change jobs many times, and you'll need the skills to adapt and learn. Your learning won't stop at college graduation.

Exercise your mind

Just as sports and exercise strengthen your body and health, education strengthens your mind and intellect. You should be using school *to learn how to learn: to exercise your mental muscles.* It's like doing intellectual sit-ups.

You already know about the value of physical exercise. Let's look at a student who just sits around a lot, who has never played sports, has never exercised, and has eaten junk food and played computer games all his life. At age 18, he is told that his life suddenly depends on running the hurdles in an upcoming track event. What are the chances he will win the race? What are the chances he will even clear the first hurdle?

But runners who have been training for these hurdles throughout high school will sail over them because they're in shape and they know how. So it is with learning: Exercising your mind in high school gets it into shape for the academic and career hurdles ahead.

Be college smart. *"But,"* you say, *"I have a friend who knows 'this person' who never even finished college and is a multimillionaire."* There's no question that some part of life depends on luck. A few people win the lottery. Most don't. If you just sit around waiting for "good fortune," you'll waste a lot of time that you might spend creating your future.

How important is your education today?

Since you'll have to spend most of your life as a learner, you might as well get learning under control. If you do, you'll find the other parts of your life will be a lot easier and more enjoyable. Plus, your education will take on a very practical and personal meaning for you.

High grades in college-prep courses, high academic achievement, an excellent high school record, a distinctive extracurricular effort, and enthusiastic letters of recommendation from teachers — all these translate into more than honors, awards, and getting into the college you want. They translate into prospects for your future, a great feeling of achievement, confidence, enjoyment, excitement, personal stability, and, yes, money. Money? In college you could be eligible for grants and scholarships (money you don't have to pay back) and financial aid (low-interest loans). Later, in life, successful students typically build strong earning potential (a salary) for themselves.

You could say this book is about taking control: control of your education, and, ultimately, your whole life. And the more control you have of your education, the more control you have of your future. Get serious! **Be college smart.** Your life depends on it.

PSST! Read the highlights. They will give you a quick overview of why knowing how to learn is so important to your life. If you thought learning was something that you did only while you sat in a classroom, you're mistaken. For your generation, it's a major life skill.

What kind of student are you *really*?
(No cheating!)

You probably know many kinds of students. Some really know what they are doing. Others do not. Still others are putting on a good show, but when the going gets tough, they lack the concentration and the determination to keep going. Here's a chance for you think about yourself as a student. In this chapter, you'll meet three types of students. Which one are you?

If you are reading this guidebook, you're already serious — or you're getting serious — about your education. That's already a major step. You're realizing how important your education is to your life, and you're starting to think about *where you want it to take you*. One place is college. Getting there *and succeeding there:* both are serious business.

How serious do you need to be? Well, "serious" doesn't mean you suddenly lose the fun in your life or become a different person. It means you take control of your days so you can do everything you *need* and *want to do*. It means becoming an independent and capable student who improves day by day.

Serious students are going places

Students are people who are supposed to learn and get the highest grades they can. Each day, your grades on tests and assignments determine your final grades. Your final grades help determine your future.

- Will you get into the college that's right for you?
- Will you get into that interesting or challenging college program?
- Will you get into a college that leads to the career path you want?

The plain fact is that what you do every day as a student (listening carefully in class, following directions, completing assignments, meeting deadlines, studying with concentration, and earning good grades) has really far-reaching effects. That's why getting serious is so important.

Plus, if you think about it, what you do now, as a student, mirrors what you will do as an adult: going off to work each day, doing a job according to someone's directions, meeting the demands of others, and trying to succeed by using your mind. School is like a job where you are paid in grades and knowledge.

The demands of school also teach you *to become a productive person.* All those assignments, tests, projects, lab reports, and papers teach you how to get things done. Productive people are always in high demand: Colleges are eager to accept productive students, and, later, employers are eager to offer them jobs. Your grades are important, but as a student, grades are only one measure of your productivity.

Look around you at other students in school. Then ask yourself, "*Who will be successful in life? Who won't?*" Why do you put some students in the "successful" category but not others? You can tell by their everyday actions: Those students who are serious about their education get things done and are going somewhere. They're moving ahead. They're better organized, and they are more successful at what they try.

What about you? What will your friends say when they are asked if *you* will be successful? Your friends will judge your seriousness of purpose, not how much fun you are. Successful students are in control of themselves. They get things done: from day to day, from semester to semester, and from year to year. They're focused and *balanced* (which means they still have fun). They envision a successful and exciting life for themselves. They plan ahead. They set and reach goals because they're going places.

This guidebook gives you Strategies do all of these things — to succeed now and in the future.

The Strategies really work

For more than 25 years, I have advised and counseled all kinds of college students. The Strategies in this guidebook come from my experience talking and working with thousands of students —

- Students trying to keep on track
- Students struggling with grades
- Students trying to climb out of deep academic holes
- Students with great ambitions
- Students who couldn't get a handle on their ambitions
- Students who were overwhelmed but who were trying hard to succeed

As you go through this guidebook, you may find that you already have some Strategies under control. That's great. Often, just knowing that you are doing the right thing can be reassuring. However, other Strategies may be new to you. Still others, you might not take too seriously until you read through them and understand their importance.

All the Strategies are important. Practicing and perfecting them in high school will put you in control of your life and your courses. And when you get to college, the Strategies will make you successful, less stressed, more confident, and focused. Most importantly, because you've mastered using the Strategies, you'll be among those students who graduate *on time*.

Want to be rich and famous?

Lots of teens do. Certainly, these are high goals. But if you asked these teens *how* they are going to achieve this fame and fortune, you may find their "strategies" more than a bit vague.

Let's return to our mountain-climbing analogy for a moment. If you're a student who is serious about succeeding, you need to look at the entire mountain. You should be thinking about reaching the peak and enjoying the view from the top. But some climbers only watch the path that's right in front of them or the rock that they are crawling over at that moment. To figure out what kind of climber/student you are, put a checkmark next to the section below that best describes your attitude toward your classes. Be honest! For now, don't worry about the three labels. You need to know who you are *at this moment*. You can always change.

□ **Clueless Student.** If you are a Clueless Student, school is something to "get through" and "leave behind." You find school dull. You're waiting for the excitement to begin, but it never seems to arrive. You think of your education in terms of compartments. You move from one course to the next, one semester to the next, one year to the next, until you've finished another phase of your education. Then you move on to the next phase, expecting it to be just like the last.

You don't really exert yourself. Nor do you look too far ahead — the future is not something you think about. Your goal is to work just enough to get an "okay" grade but not to do more work than you have to. Mostly, you're content with getting by, and sometimes that means getting a pretty good grade for doing only a satisfactory job. Getting an occasional bad grade is okay with you. Reaching for a long-term goal is not something you think about. You're willing to trust to luck or fate that things will work out.

□ **Typical Student.** If you are a Typical Student, you work harder than a Clueless Student. You put forth effort — but only when you want to. You study for tests and complete assignments, but then you often draw a line: You don't work at courses that you don't like or that you find too hard or too boring. In general, you earn high grades, but basically, you work for grades, not knowledge. You have no real sense of how all of your courses fit together. There's no BIG picture for you. What's more, like a Clueless Student, you don't think about how high school classes prepare you for college and what you might do in life.

Most college-bound high school students belong to this group. The number of great or good grades earned by these students changes from semester to semester, depending on how many courses they "like." Unfortunately, Typical Students never achieve great success because when courses get too tough, these students back off and settle for a "whatever" grade, satisfied that they've given their courses "a good shot."

☐ **College Smart Student.** If you are a College Smart Student, you are a serious student. You understand that your education is more than something to "get through" and "leave behind." That distinguishes you from a Clueless Student right away. And unlike a Typical Student, you work for *all* of your courses.

You get high grades, but you know that **grades are not the real goal. There's a larger purpose:** *filling your knowledge bank, developing learning skills, and achieving certain academic goals.* You are looking beyond classes, semesters, and grades. You're trying to figure out *where this education is going to take you.* Even though your life goals may be a bit hazy and change over time, you're still always thinking ahead. For example, you might say to yourself: *I like math. I wonder if I would like engineering or business. I like language and literature. I wonder if I would make a good lawyer.* You're beginning to understand how academic success actually creates many opportunities for your life. You are continually working with possible goals in mind, thinking about the future. A College Smart Student has the maturity to see the BIG picture.

What is the BIG picture?

- Every course you take develops your mind in a different way.

- Courses relate to each other. They merge to form a whole. An education is *not* lots of little compartments, separate courses, or separate semesters.

- Neglecting one academic area for another shortchanges you.

- Knowledge brings opportunities in college and the world.

- Initiative and planning are needed to get through the challenges that arise in high school *and* the greater challenges of college.

Use this guidebook — tuck it in your backpack.

To achieve success, you must be a college smart student. You become this student by using the Strategies in this guidebook.

As you get better at using these Strategies, you will believe that anything is possible — you can reach any goal, carry out any plan, and fulfill any ambition. You'll find that your courses become more interesting, even exciting. You can achieve high grades and feel the confidence that comes with great personal success, the result of your good effort. But even more exciting is the idea that you are beginning to make a life for yourself. When you graduate from high school, you'll be prepared to choose the right college, then the right area of study, and, eventually, the right career.

You'll know, how to use your mind and energy to take control of not only your days and education but also your future.

All three types of college-bound students described in this chapter graduate from high school. They get into college. But getting into college is one thing. Succeeding in college is much harder. However, if you are a college smart student, you've developed knowledge and learning skills that will open many college opportunities to you. With your strong background, you'll be able to take all kinds of college courses, and each one will be more interesting, satisfying, and exciting than the last *because you have developed the maturity, knowledge, and vision to succeed.*

And that last thought is very important. **YOU'RE THE ONE** who has to make choices about your life and your education. Which student are you? Which student do you want to be?

PSST! Now that you know about the three kinds of students and how the BIG picture works, review the highlights — so you really see how all those ideas fit together. You have some decisions to make, and the decision you make now will seriously affect your success in college and in life. Make good ones, and you're on your way!

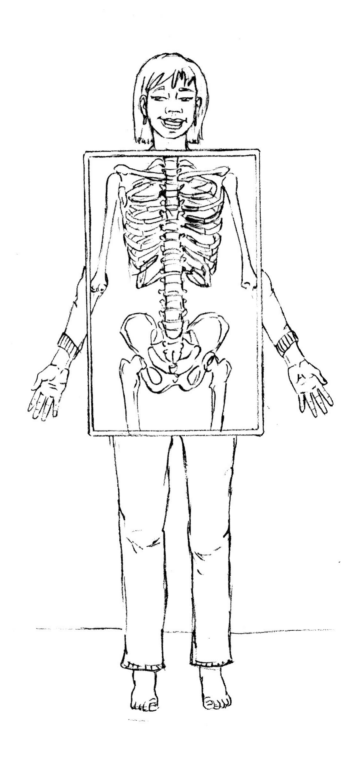

The person inside the student
(You're not just bones and organs.)

Here's another chance to find out more about yourself. The more you know about yourself, the better student you'll be. This section helps you think about yourself in new ways. You are more complicated than you know!

Take a closer look at yourself. To get your mind warmed up, work on these questions. They will help you zero in on yourself as a student.

1) What's most important to you? *Rank each aspect of your life using a scale of 1 to 5.* (5 is most important to you, and 1 is least important.)

   ___ your health   ___ your part-time job

   ___ your education   ___ your social life

   ___ your athletics   ___ your family

2) Regarding school in general, *circle the letter of the description that **best applies** to you as a student.*

   a) a student who enjoys everything about school — always has, probably always will

   b) a student with strong likes and dislikes about school: teachers, courses, studying, tests

   c) a student who likes school as long as it teaches practical skills that lead to your personal goals

   d) a student who finds school less and less interesting as you get older

3) As a student, how would you describe yourself? *Circle the letter for only one answer.*

   a) a student who earns *all* high grades and works to keep them high

   b) a student with *mostly* high grades, but not always

   c) a student whose grades could probably use a good "jump-start"

   d) a student who would rather not think that much about grades

4) If academic achievement and good grades are important to you, why?
   Rank each statement using a scale of 1 to 5. (5 is most important to you, and 1 is least important.)

   ___ You find academic achievement (learning) personally satisfying.

   ___ You enjoy the admiration of teachers, family, and friends.

   ___ You look forward to the potential for financial reward later in life.

   ___ You like collecting academic awards (honors, scholarships, etc.).

   ___ You look forward to moving to a higher level of education or into a career.

Keep your answers in mind as you read the rest of this chapter. In a few pages, you'll see what you've just learned about yourself.

Being a student isn't the only thing you have to do!

Do you understand yourself as a person? As a student? Do you think about such things? Knowing more about yourself as a person makes you smarter about how to live your days — and your life. The better you understand yourself as a student, the better your education and your life will be. So let's get to know you better.

First, let's take a big step back and look at your whole life, beginning with all the roles you play as a person:

- Son/Daughter (Parents won't let you forget THAT role.)
- Brother/Sister (That's a role you might want to forget now and then.)
- Athlete (Go team!)
- Best Friend (Hey, what's new?)
- Boyfriend/Girlfriend (Ahhhh!)
- Employee (I'll get right to it.)
- Club/Group Member (Let's do a fundraiser!)
- Musician/Artist (Beautiful!)
- Religious Person (Silence.)
- Computer-Game Player, TV Watcher, Hobbyist, etc. (Just relax.)

You might not regularly think about these roles, but when you do, you discover that your life is filled with activities linked to all the roles you play. How do you feel about these many roles? Some, you love. Some, you don't. Some, you hardly ever think about until you're asked, like now.

Be college smart. You're a complex person, and life asks a lot of responsibility from you. Even if you weren't a student, your days and weeks would be filled with activity. Add your life as a student, and you start to wonder how you can manage it all. But it's no longer a matter of "if" you can. You have to. And you have to figure out how, BEFORE YOU GET TO COLLEGE.

You're at that point in life when you cannot just sit back and watch life go by. Yet you can't just dive in and let it sweep you up and toss you around like some roaring river, either. Are the waters in your river rough or calm? Are you just floating along, or barely staying on top of the water? It's time to take control. So that no matter how fast, rough, or deep the river, you can still get from one place to the next — and not just any old place, but specific destinations (goals) that you choose for yourself.

In the river of your life, you need a boat — a sturdy and reliable one. And right now that boat is your education. It will get you from here to there. Can you steer the boat? Can you navigate the boat so it gets you where you want to go, even the short trips? What about the long trips? Where do you want this boat to take you in life? To travel safely, you have to know how to be the captain of your boat.

To be the best student you can, or to be the captain of your educational boat, you must —

- make sensible decisions.
- manage your responsibilities.
- organize your time.
- set goals.
- evaluate your progress.
- be aware of your achievements.

That's a lot, I know. Just take a look at one of your typical days. Use the **Weekly Activity Map** that follows. Choose any school day (just one for now), and fill in each hour of your day from 7:00 a.m. to 11:00 p.m. Be accurate and honest. Take some time on this. You may find that because your activities are not neatly divided into hours, certain boxes in your day may contain more than one activity. Here are some ideas to get you started.

_____ Put in your class hours.

_____ Add the hours you usually study.

_____ Mark the hours you watch TV or are on your computer.

_____ Record naps, long phone calls, or any time hanging out with friends.

_____ Don't forget hours you spend working a part-time job, practicing with your team, playing your musical instrument, or volunteering.

_____ List the times that you eat.

_____ Include times you spend just relaxing.

Weekly Activity Map

	M	T	W	T	F	S	S
7:00							
8:00							
9:00							
10:00							
11:00							
12:00							
1:00							
2:00							
3:00							
4:00							
5:00							
6:00							
7:00							
8:00							
9:00							
10:00							
11:00							
	go to bed	*go to bed*	*go to bed*	*go to bed*	*go to bed*	*go to bed*	*go to bed*
TOTAL							

Where your time goes

When you've finished, you'll have a visual map of your busy day. Surprised by the number of things you do in 16 hours? Checking out what you do in one day tells you a lot about how you use your time. For the hours that you are in school, you're required to be in certain places — classes, labs, study halls. If you have a job, that time is also planned for you. Are you an athlete? Better get to practice. How many hours in your day are really yours to decide on?

You're becoming more mature, and your life is changing. Becoming mature means taking on more responsibilities, whether or not you want to. You have to start acting more like a person who is leaving behind the impulsive habits of a child. When you grow out of those childish habits, you can become the captain of your boat. You begin to learn how to read maps, plot a course, navigate the boat, and make decisions. If you just let the water take you wherever it's going, you might not like the places when you get there.

Being a "captain" means that you recognize that all your life roles are important, including your student role — and you manage them. Yet the student role is the one that too many teens treat like an annoying brother or sister. Yes, your education can be demanding, even annoying: all those different courses, teachers, tests, and homework assignments. But like your brother or sister, your education is not going away. It better not, because your life depends on it.

The learning skills you develop and the information you accumulate in school will help you throughout your life. As an adult, you'll be a person who is interested in all kinds of things, and these interests will prevent you from ever being "bored." Plus, learners make great employees. Learners are intelligent and creative, always looking for better opportunities — just as employers are always looking for employees who can learn new jobs and do them with creativity. Learners are versatile people. They find that moving from one job to another is easy. And because employers value them, learners can "pay" their way in life. Having knowledge helps you become a person who owns a car, a house, and all the items that fill houses.

In short, your education is the boat that gets you to many destinations on the river of life. But acquiring an education takes intelligence, stamina, and a respect for what you're doing.

Be college smart. When you are older and have a career, your job will take up much of your day. Right now, your job is being a student. And you have to treat that responsibility like someone who is employed and is getting paid for your efforts. Because that's exactly what's happening: You *are* going to be paid for your efforts. Your pay is the kind of exciting future you make for yourself.

Looking at the bigger picture

Jobs demand time, skill, and effort. If you look at your student role as a job, you have to look at a whole work week to really see what's going on. So now it's time to fill out the rest of your week to create a weekly activity map that shows you how you use all your waking hours. Filling in a week's worth of activities is going to take you a little while, but filling in the boxes honestly will take you a long way to understanding yourself not only as a student, *but as a person with many responsibilities that must be managed along with academic ones.* (Don't neglect using the weekends. You live in a 7-day week.)

Directions. Finish filling in the **Weekly Activity Map**. Record everything you do during a week's time. Fill in all the hours.

- Add up the hours you spend on each activity and put those totals in the blanks below.

- The blanks in the last row are for other activities that take time in your week but are not listed, like household chores.

- Total the hours you spend studying each day. Record them on the blank below each day on the **Weekly Activity Map**.

_____ in class	_____ on the job	_____ TV time	_____ computer time
_____ study time	_____ sports time	_____ socializing	_____ relaxing
_____ music/art	_____ hobbies	_____ eating	_____ family
_____ other	_____ other	_____ other	_____ other

Are you surprised by how much time you spend on some of these roles? Think about the time you spend being a boyfriend or girlfriend — and that includes phone conversations and online time. Did you imagine that you really spend that much time on email? Or on the athletic field? Or playing computer games, watching TV, or listening to music? Now that you've accurately described your week, keep it in mind as you read on.

A note about your Weekly Activity Map

If you filled in the boxes pretty easily, that means two things: (1) You already have a fairly good idea of how you spend your time and (2) you have some pattern to your life. You're off to a good start. Other students who say *"I don't know — I do different things at different times, depending on how I feel"* have got a ways to go.

Why time is important

Think about this. A good competitive college, one that will give you an education worth the large amount of money you'll be paying, would expect you to study at least 30 hours a week as a freshman.

So let's work backwards. In order to be ready for that 30-hour challenge, you should be studying at least 25 hours a week as a high school senior, 20 hours as a junior, 15 hours as a sophomore, and 10 hours as a freshman. Are you doing that? If you're not, you're not going to be ready for college, **no matter what your grades are now.** Get used to putting in the time for study. If you don't, you'll be one of those students who starts college but

a) needs extra years to earn a degree,
b) loses his or her career dreams because courses were "too hard," or
c) fails to graduate.

Are you a straight-*A* student? Why not? You're too old to say that lower grades happen because *you're "just not good in a certain subject."* Grades are as much a matter of time and effort as they are of talent. If a subject is harder for you, do you study it more? If you know yourself, you'll know which subjects need more time. We'll talk more about the subject of learning and time in Strategies 7 and 8.

Fitting it all in — it's up to you

Let's put things together. The point is that knowing yourself is important: whether you're a very good student who wants to stay that way or a student who needs to take better control of time. Recognize all the roles you play in life and how they fill your day. If you want to improve as a student, you have to control not only your student role, but your other roles as well.

That's why we began by looking at a typical day for you. Your high school organizes the first part. You organize the second part. Or do you? Are you the kind of student who takes control of your time? Or do you just let things "happen"? Do you scramble to get in assignments? Do you meet most (but not all) of your deadlines? Do you use time well to prepare for the next test? Or do you cram the day before?

As you filled out your **Weekly Activity Map**, carefully recording everything you do in an entire week, from morning to night, what did you find out about yourself overall? How about yourself as a student? Are you giving that role the time and effort it requires? How close are you to meeting the study-time goals listed above in the **Why time is important** section?

The BIG QUESTION we are trying to answer is this: *Do you control your week, or does it control you?* When you were filling out your Activity Map and realized that you would have to include homework/study time, did you start thinking about the need to add more time to your after-school student role? Or were those hours already assigned because you are the captain of your educational boat — or at least the first mate?

Do you see how we're getting closer and closer to understanding how well you know yourself as a student?

Sleep or die! (Well, almost!)

Don't forget the importance of the hours of your day that are NOT included on your schedule sheet: from 11:00 p.m. to 7:00 a.m. During these hours, you should be sleeping. Eating healthy is important, exercising is important, but *sleeping is essential.*

If you don't eat right or keep your body in shape, you'll feel the consequences, but not right away. If you don't sleep enough, you'll feel it tomorrow or the day after. Lack of sleep is deadly to a student. Sleep deprivation, as doctors call it, makes your mind wander and even shut down at times. It makes understanding or remembering new information difficult, if not impossible.

Isn't your main job as a student to use your mind? Absolutely. So don't do anything that makes your mind weak. Sleeplessness will do just that. Using your mind in all your various courses is hard enough, even when you're rested.

And some people need more sleep than others. Figure it out for yourself. It's easy to do. Try this: Get a normal 8 hours each night for two to three nights in a row (and that's absolutely the minimum) and ask yourself, *"Am I tired during the first two classes of my day?"* If so, go to bed earlier for the next two to three nights. How do you feel after getting more sleep for a few nights? Adjust your schedule to get the amount of sleep your body needs.

A late night here and there won't kill you. But too many will. One more thing: Don't deceive yourself about playing "catch-up" with sleep by staying up late during the week and sleeping all weekend. It doesn't work.

If you get into bad sleeping habits in high school, you'll mostly likely carry them to college. Dorm life invites staying up late talking, listening to music, socializing, or playing computer games. These late nights mean that students often sleep on and off during the day to make up their lost sleep, sometimes sleeping through their classes — in or out of the classroom. The next night, the cycle repeats itself.

Start working on good sleeping habits now: GET ENOUGH SLEEP!

Controlling time is a BIG DEAL.

For some of you, filling out your **Weekly Activity Map** was probably difficult, maybe even frustrating. However, filling out a chart like the Activity Map is the best way to see just how busy you are.

Knowing what you do each hour of each day is the first step to learning about yourself as a person — and *as a student.* This understanding lies at the heart of your ability to succeed academically. Despite all the things you do and all the roles you play, you should always remind yourself, *"I am a student, and I give time and energy to those things that lead to my academic success."*

Question: *Is being a student important to you?* If you plan on being a student for several more years, becoming a skilled learner is VERY IMPORTANT, whether or not you know it now. So if you are going to college, the answer is *"Yes, being a student is important to me."*

Whatever kind of student you are right now, you should know this: **Learning takes time, and therefore, to be a learner, you have to make time for learning.** That's how education becomes important in your life. To make time for learning, you have to control your personal time each day and each week. Remember that learning and going to school are your full-time job, requiring effort and responsibility every day.

So as you looked at your **Weekly Activity Map**, what did you discover about yourself *as a student?* Did you find that you don't have all that much time to study? Are your days so packed that activities squeeze out study time?

Remember the BIG QUESTION: Are you controlling your days and weeks, or are they controlling you? One of the major reasons that students don't succeed in college is that they cannot control their days and make time for study. Those are your two most important goals: making time for study and then using that time to study.

Before you can put in the time, you have to *find* the time. Your **Weekly Activity Map** may have shown you that you should simplify or organize your life. If your days are too packed, you'll have to clear away some "things" to open up time for study. That's taking control. And you're the only one who CAN control your days. And what will surprise you is that when you control your days, you'll feel better about yourself — now and in your college years. (We'll talk more about this in Strategy 8.) Keep in mind that your job as a student will become more, rather than less, demanding year after year.

Learning to control time now is the way you navigate your educational boat toward college. It's a skill you'll need because the daily responsibilities that lie ahead of you are really big. Start now. Keep looking inside yourself and at your days. Pay close attention to your student role and keep developing as a student. Your job is to make sure that you make enough time in your days for one of the most important parts of your life: your education.

What's a perfect student?

There are good students and bad ones — and many kinds of students in between. But is there a "perfect" student? You already know students who really have it "together." (Maybe it's you!) How would you describe this student? Look at the words below.

Ambitious	Creative	Inquisitive	Private
Argumentative	Determined	Lazy	Respectful
Calm	Disagreeable	Motivated	Serious
Careless	Energetic	Moody	Shy
Casual	Friendly	Nervous	Sociable
Conceited	Generous	Organized	Stubborn
Confident	Honest	Patient	Talkative
Cooperative	Immature	Practical	Unfocused

Now write in the spaces of the two columns the words that best describe the "perfect" and "worst" student.

Characteristics of the "perfect" student	Characteristics of the "worst" student
1. _____	1. _____
2 _____	2. _____
3 _____	3. _____
4. _____	4. _____
5. _____	5. _____

How about you?

The first question to ask yourself is this: Do the words you've listed for your perfect student include qualities that you already have? Or are these qualities that you'd *like* to have? Give this some thought.

Then consider this. How does each of the five qualities you've chosen for the perfect student help the student achieve and succeed? What about the words from the worst-student list? How do these qualities prevent student success? Answer these two questions, and you'll begin to see that how you live your life as a *person* affects your life as a *student.*

You may have noticed that some of the descriptive words in the list are not clear. For example —

- Being casual is not bad in itself, but being so casual that you become disorganized will mean you can't manage all the material you're supposed to learn in all your courses.

- Being stubborn can be bad if you don't listen to others who are trying to help you, but being stubborn can be good if it means you don't give up on subjects that are hard for you.

- Being quiet is not bad, unless it keeps you from talking with teachers and counselors.

- Being energetic is great, unless that energy leads to nervousness or distracts you in class.

- Being talkative is good if it gives you the confidence to take part in class discussions, but if you're talking to your friends instead of listening to the teacher, being talkative moves into the "worst" student column.

These sometimes-good, sometimes-bad words just describe personalities. As the examples show, how you use these characteristics in particular situations determines whether they are good or bad.

If you were to ask your teachers which qualities they would like to see — not only in you but in all their students — what would they say? Well, think about when the class bell rings. Teachers want everyone seated and prepared for class, with notebooks open and pens in hand, and interested. Right? These actions represent qualities: *determined, organized, motivated, serious,* and *courteous.* These words are clear, and they don't depend on circumstances.

The characteristics of a perfect student, like the ones we just mentioned, are really the same characteristics an employer looks for in an employee. They fall into three general categories: (1) skills and talents, (2) personal traits, (3) qualities of character. What do these mean? Well, just think about it. Pretend that you are hiring someone. First you look at applications. But they can tell you very little, so you conduct interviews. You want to meet people face to face, so you can ask them questions.

What do you want to discover in an interview? You've got it: Their skills and talents, their personal traits, and their qualities of character. Why? Just think about it for minute.

- **You naturally want someone who can do the job,** so you want to know about their skills and talents, their educational background as it relates to the job, and their success in previous jobs.

- **You want a person who will get along with you and other employees,** so you want to size up their personal traits, like friendliness, cheerfulness, and kindness.

- **And you want a person with high moral standards** — qualities of character like honesty and responsibility.

If teachers could interview students for their courses, teachers would do just the same. They would want students who have a good educational background with high grades in other courses; students who get along with other students, so the classroom work is pleasant; and, of course, students who are honest, hard working, and dependable.

Want to take describing the perfect student to the next step? You might want to ask each of your teachers and your guidance counselor which five characteristics they would use to describe you. Or if you don't want the question to be so personal, ask these people if they would give you the five basic qualities they would like to see in all students. If the words they give you aren't already on the list you've made, add them to your list. It takes a lot more than five characteristics to make up a perfect student. Now you have a list that identifies the qualities you want to practice and develop.

Be college smart. The point of all this is to get you thinking very precisely about the kind of student you are. But here's a warning. If you were asked to choose five words to describe yourself as a student *right now,* and some words were good and some were not so good, the last thing you should do is sit back and say, *"Well, that's just the way I am!"* Remember, qualities like being organized, thorough, or careful are *learned.* They take effort, the same kind of practice as shooting free throws. Saying, *"That's the way I am"* allows you to give up. It's just an excuse for not trying to develop the qualities you need to succeed as a student. Have confidence that you can develop the qualities of a perfect student — a college smart student — because, with practice, you can!

Your qualities affect your future.

College applications will ask you to write essays about yourself and explain why you're the kind of student that will significantly contribute to College X or University Z. They will, you know.

It's hard to be truthful if you are generally uncommunicative, disorganized, and unmotivated as a student. Or imagine yourself in a job interview after college. You'll want to describe yourself to the interviewer as the right person to hire. You say you are determined, organized, and energetic. Will an interviewer ask, *"How do you explain some of these low grades or withdrawals from courses? Why did you attend four colleges before completing your bachelor's degree? Why did it take you six and a half years?"*

Right now, college, career, and adulthood seem so far away, but they're just around the corner. You have to start getting ready for it all now.

What you've just learned about yourself

These activities have just helped you answer several questions about yourself and the kind of student you are.

- Think about how you answered the questions in this chapter. Your answers will tell you how much you value school and how seriously you take your education.

- Look at your **Weekly Activity Map**. It tells you how many roles you are juggling and how much room you are now making for education in your life.

- Examine your word list. It gives you the opportunity to compare yourself to the perfect student and gives you direction to set some personal goals.

All of your answers directly or indirectly describe your attitude toward learning in one way or another. As you go over these activities, ask yourself, *"Is this the student I want to be?"* Are there areas you want to improve?

If you still say, *"So what's the big deal?"* stay tuned. You'll find out — IT'S A VERY BIG DEAL. Defining yourself as a student is a very important step toward defining yourself as a one-of-a-kind, independent person.

 PSST! This chapter is all about you. Now that you've read through this chapter from start to finish, go over the highlights. This is very important information. Are there changes that you want to make? How "in charge of yourself" are you?

How you gain independence and control
(You might be surprised.)

When you look ahead to your future, what is it that you want? To be yourself and to determine your own future — a future that might include a career, success, and personal happiness. You can achieve such things only if you have control over your own life. But what gets in the way? Your education! Or at least it seems like it. You may feel that you're never in control of yourself at school. You have teachers telling you what to do. Parents telling you. Counselors telling you. Where's the independence or control in that? It's there. You just have to be able to see it. Read on!

The truth is that you don't just suddenly become *in control and independent.* Rather, as you grow in intelligence and maturity, life gives you ways to practice these skills and get better at using them. The key word here is *practice.* You must practice these skills to master them. Where do you get the chance? At school! Your education gives you dozens of opportunities to juggle responsibilities — to practice being independent, in control, and productive. Don't believe it? Think about it this way:

- In high school, your teachers decide what you must learn in a class, *but you control how and when to fit learning into your days.*

- Your high school tells you that you need certain requirements to graduate, *but you have to figure out how to manage and succeed in all those courses every day.*

- Your school insists that you take a variety of courses, *but you have to find ways to train your mind to do different kinds of thinking and learning to succeed in courses that can be very different from each other.*

You say these examples don't make you free enough? How free do you want to be? Free like your parents? Good. Let's see how free they are.

About adult freedom

When you were very young, you always thought that your parents were totally free and in control of their lives. But don't they, too, have bosses, work schedules, deadlines, projects, and assignments at work? (Doesn't that sound like school?) If you take managing your independence seriously, the kinds of decisions you make every day in school will prepare you to gradually enter and succeed in adulthood. What you should now understand is a more real definition of freedom: **finding new ways to meet challenges within the boundaries that life gives you.**

So after the midpoint of your educational life (middle school), you're the one in charge. Your future will be the result of your decisions. No more hand holding. From now on, more and more of the decisions are entirely up to you, and they're decisions that can't be ignored. The right choices help you move ahead with your life. You're the one who decides what kind of student you will be, and why. As you move through each phase of your education, you'll have to take ownership and say, *"They were MY decisions, good and bad."*

What grades mean to your freedom and your future

You know the record of your grades in the school office? (This record is called a *transcript*.) I want you think of it as your savings account. What do you do with your savings account? If you're smart, you work to earn money, and then you deposit the money in your savings account. When you need money to buy something, the money is there for you. You spend carefully. You also continue to save for the future.

What happens if you don't work very hard and earn very much? When you want to buy something, you can't. You don't have enough money.

It's the same with the grades on your school record, your transcript. Really great grades give you power and help you buy what you need. **Are your grades really like money? Yes, you use your grades to purchase your future.** Remember the question that your family members always ask you: *"How are you doing in school?"* That question changes as you get older and as you move closer to college, your hoped-for career, and your adulthood. The question becomes *"How DID you do in school?"* And it's asked by a stranger who can alter your life: college admissions counselor, college financial-aid officer, or, later on, potential employer.

By looking at your transcript, these people will determine whether you may move from here to there, from this level to that — from high school to certain colleges, from college to a job or more schooling. And with electronic information, the transcript of each stage of your education will be readily available to the people who need to review it.

Your transcript tells these people quite a lot about you. If your transcript shows high grades in all your courses, the evaluator will conclude that you are a steady, serious student. Therefore, your transcript can earn you a seat in the freshman class of your favorite college. If your grades are up and down and all over the place, your "academic savings account" won't have enough money to earn you the college or job that you want. If your grades are high only in easy courses but fall in harder courses, the evaluator will recognize that you don't work as a student. And that brings up another point about academic savings accounts.

Not all grades are equal in the eyes of a reviewer. Reviewers don't look just at your grade point average. They look at individual grades. Did you earn that *A* in Physical Education or Physics? If you take courses that prepare you for college and that are challenging, an excellent grade becomes all the more impressive. It's good as gold. If you are taking really easy courses (just earning enough credits to graduate), your transcript is less impressive. Yes, you may have more *A*s, but if you've earned them in less-demanding courses, they are "worth" less in the eyes of the reviewer. They "buy" less of a future for you.

Here's the point: Students often think grades are relevant only in the present, or maybe the near future. Not so. Reviewers are frequently looking at your academic record. Inconsistent grades tell reviewers about lapses in knowledge, initiative, dedication, responsibility, or mental agility. These are the things that colleges, professional schools (law, business, dentistry, medicine, etc.), and conscientious employers look for. "Average" grades in "average courses" damage your academic advancement, causing your future success to fade and, in some cases, disappear altogether.

When you work hard to get the best possible grades in all your courses (not just the ones you like or the easy ones), it means you are looking seriously at your future, perhaps for the first time. That makes some students a little bit nervous. Right now, as a student looking at your future, what do you see? Anything? Everything? Are you starting to see connections between academic success and future success? Read on!

Information, not grades

But here's an idea that might surprise you. Knowledge and learning are more important than grades. It's true. Grades are only supposed to signal *that* you've learned — that the information you've read in books and studied in class is now in your head.

Yet grades don't always mean that. For many students, grades represent only superficial learning and temporary knowledge. How can that be? It happens this way: Students cram for a unit test, they get a good grade, and then they move on to the next unit. They cram for the next unit test and all the others that follow. Why are they cramming? Because they didn't make time to study the material every day and really absorb it. It's all connected to time and how you use it each day.

Cramming is dangerous because it fails to create long-term knowledge (and fails to develop the learning skills you need for college). Six weeks after students finish the unit, the information they crammed right before the test evaporates. It's gone for good.

A few years later, in college, for example, a professor expects students to have a solid background in a foreign language course because of students' high school background in the language. But the knowledge isn't in their heads anymore. Crammers have no foundation to build on. They've forgotten it. As college students, they find themselves lost and scrambling in the early days of the course. College courses move quickly. As the weeks go by, students find their situation gets worse and worse — and leads to disastrous results with far-reaching consequences. Remember: Huge numbers of college freshmen don't return to campus. Huge numbers of college students can't graduate on time. **They didn't know that mapping out and managing their high school days would affect them for THE REST OF THEIR LIVES.**

The rest of this book will show you how to become a student who never has to face this problem. Oh, and by the way, one more *really important* thing you should know about grades: If you learn to study well in all your courses, you never have to worry about good grades. Once you've nailed the material, great grades can't help but follow. **Learn the material, and grades take care of themselves.**

 PSST! You want independence, and this chapter tells you that you have plenty of opportunity to take charge. Review the highlights. How you map out your days and use your time will help you build your future. You have the freedom to make these decisions!

Some pointers on using the Strategies
(Jump-start your new academic life.)

*A Message from Dr. Bob: I'm going to coach you through each of the Strategies, but before we start, I want to give you some general pointers. To get a feel for how the Strategies work together, read quickly through all of them first. Then start with whatever ones you want or need most. Add more as you go. During the school year, help yourself stay on track by reading and rereading the Strategies often. Gradually, you will see how they all fit together. The Strategies help you map out your approach to your days — and your future. You'll soon become the college smart student you want and **need** to be.*

As you read each Strategy, remind yourself of these six important facts (and reread them often):

1. **The more Strategies you use, the better results you will achieve.** The more Strategies you use, the stronger you become as a student compared to other students, even other **straight-A** students.

2. **It's never too late to start.** No matter where you are in your high school career, start using these Strategies now so you're ready to handle college later on. That's where the going really gets tougher.

3. **Believe in the Strategies.** I have seen the Strategies work with all kinds of students. They either kept their grades high as courses got tougher or they improved their grades.

4. **You, not anyone else, are in charge of your education.** When you walk into any class for the first day, remember that your challenge is the course material, not the school, not the teacher, not the other students. These are all factors in your learning, but when you come right down to it, learning the course material is in your hands.

5. **You don't have to love school, your courses, or your teachers — or other students, for that matter.** You just have to take your education seriously, respect it, and give it the time it deserves. It is, after all, the pathway to your future.

6. **You need to practice these skills *before* you get to college.** You may think that you're doing all right as a student just the way you are. Your grades are pretty good, and you get them without too much effort. You may even get those grades with "temporary knowledge" — learning enough to pass a test but then forgetting what you've learned. Cramming is a habit that will really hurt you in college.

In college, earning good grades is much harder. It requires more effort, more time, and greater skill. I promise you: You will need these Strategies to succeed. It's a promise that grows out of listening to thousands of college students *who also had good high school experiences but ran into trouble in college.* They didn't have the skills to manage the load.

The way to prepare for college is to use high school as practice. High school is your training ground for succeeding in college.

These are the Strategies in the next part of the book.

Strategy 1 — How, exactly to "use your head"

Strategy 2 — Your study place

Strategy 3 — The first two weeks

Strategy 4 — Knowing how to talk

Strategy 5 — Talking to teachers

Strategy 6 — Talking with your guidance counselor

Strategy 7 — Studying vs. homework

Strategy 8 — Creating a schedule

Strategy 9 — All about tests

Strategy 10 — Tracking grades

Strategy 11 — Extracurricular activities and recommendations, too

Strategy 12 — Setting goals

 PSST! As you work your way through the Strategies, don't forget to keep coming back to the highlights that define the bigger picture in these introductory chapters. You're climbing the mountain. As a person who is independent and in control, you're becoming a successful learner, prepared for life in college and the Information Age. The Strategies that follow show you how.

Strategy 1

How, exactly, to "use your head" —
the right way

Here's your challenge: to be alert, energetic, and self-reliant. In elementary school, teachers and your parents were there to help you when you needed it. However, with each passing year, you are expected to invest more effort and do progressively more work **on your own.** *How well you do now depends on your willpower and your effort. Keep your goal in mind: you're getting ready to handle college!*

Learn about yourself

1. In the first column below, list your courses for the semester.

2. In the "Hours Spent" column, write about how many hours (outside of class) you spend a week on each course.

3. In the column at the far right, fill in how many additional hours you think you would have to spend on each course to guarantee an *A* — and really remember the material later on.

Course	Hours Spent	Added Time for an A

Learning and time are connected.

Over the years, I have had countless conversations with college students. No matter the student, one of the first things I asked them to do was list their courses for the semester, just as you did above. Then I asked how many hours they spent on each course. (I still do this when counseling students.)

Even if I don't already know whether I'm talking to an *A*, *B*, or *C* student (or worse), I get a very good idea about their grade point average from the way they answer my question.

- The student who can answer my question without too much hesitation is probably an *A* student.

- The student who spends the most time on one or two "hard" courses and whose study time "varies" on the other courses is usually a *B* student.

- The student who says his or her study time "all depends" on the courses, the teacher, or when exams and assignments come up usually lands in the low-*B* or *C* range.

- The student who just doesn't know what to do with such a "weird" question is in real trouble.

 Be college smart. Learning takes time. You say, *"No kidding,"* but you'd be surprised how many students don't understand that learning anything thoroughly takes time. So many students just don't get it.

Why not? Remember when we talked about middle school? That's when the BIG CHANGE takes place. It's the point where students are gradually asked to learn more and more *on their own.* Students who miss that point are always expecting to learn the way they did in grade school: sit in class and let the teacher POUR KNOWLEDGE INTO SOME HOLE IN THEIR HEAD. Grade school teachers tell you what to learn and then keep practicing with you until you have learned it. Unfortunately, the teacher is doing most of the work, and students begin to believe that learning is just a matter of being in class. So if learning just "happened" in grade school, why isn't it just "happening" in high school or college? Even college? Yes, sometimes students take *a very long time* to get it: Learning takes time outside of class!

What happens when students don't take on the personal responsibility to learn? They not only get lower and lower grades, they also become discouraged and develop negative attitudes about education. They begin to look *outside themselves* for reasons that their grades are falling. First, it's the teacher. The teacher is *"too boring"* or *"too hard"* or *"doesn't like me."* Then it's the course — *"It's dumb,"* or *"I never do very well in math"* (or English, or science, etc.). Or school is *"the same old thing, day after day."*

When students blame low grades on someone or something other than themselves, they need help. On the other hand, when students understand that low grades come from "not studying enough" and then give more time and serious effort to their courses, grades always improve.

Learn more about yourself

I used to ask college students to give me three nouns to describe their minds. Over the years I've collected these words, and they reveal a lot about how students think about themselves as learners. List three words to complete this statement: *My mind is like a* _____.

1. _____

2. _____

3. _____

The words students gave me tended to fit into two categories. See if you understand what I mean. Here are several words in random order: *box, computer, jar, filing cabinet, library, container, motherboard, closet, tree, suitcase, engine, city, backpack, and musical instrument.*

Now here are the words divided into two groups: those chosen by high-achieving students and those chosen by the average-to-low achievers.

Average/Low Achievers	High Achievers
Box	Computer
Suitcase	Musical Instrument
Filing cabinet	Library
Backpack	Tree
Jar	Engine
Container	Motherboard
Closet	City

It's rather easy to see that one group thinks of their minds as places or containers. The other group sees their mind as *functioning* devices, places, or objects. Do I have to tell you which students get high grades? Students who have "place" or "container" words for their minds believe their education is something that just happens "to" them. Their minds are passive receivers (containers). They are still in a grade school mode of learning. Successful students, on the other hand, think of their minds as processors, working instruments, devices, living things, or mechanisms for actively learning and organizing information. Their minds are active and dynamic. Their college experience is exciting, fulfilling, and rewarding.

Processing in action

Walk into a classroom, sit down, and class begins. The teacher says *"Today we're going to begin Shakespeare's play* Hamlet*"* or *"Today we'll learn how to calculate the molecular weight of a chemical compound."*

Students with "processing minds" come to class prepared — having already started reading the play or already knowing something about the basics of molecular weight. These students are always working ahead of the course's schedule, ahead of the teacher. For these students —

- Class is an exchange between student and teacher.

- What the teacher talks about is never entirely new, so the class period is a real learning experience.

- Although they come to class with some knowledge of the topic, they leave class with more knowledge. The two pieces fit together. One piece builds on the other. This kind of knowledge is strengthened later that day when the student sits down to do homework and study. The student is layering on knowledge that "stays."

However, students with "container heads" wait for the teacher to talk about something that's new to them. What's more, they're hoping they will understand everything they need to know by the end of class. The information the teacher presents to the container-headed student — waiting for knowledge to be "poured in" — may or may not stay in the student's mind. The teacher may be covering quite a lot of material. For the container-minded student, class is like trying to quickly pour a lot of liquid from a bottle with a big opening into one with a smaller opening: Half the liquid ends up on the floor. And that's the way class goes for "the container students." A good deal of knowledge always ends up on the floor.

Why do I have to take this course?

Too many students think that the only purpose of education is to accumulate facts and information. Certainly, learning involves absorbing and accumulating knowledge. But learning involves much more than that.

If you're a student who grumbles that you can't see why you should study a foreign language or learn some math functions that you'll probably never use, you need an explanation. Here it is: Learning is not just gathering knowledge. It develops your mind, just like exercising your body.

Different kinds of exercise. Learning engages the mind in many kinds of thinking — from procedures in language and math, to problem-solving in the sciences, to collecting and memorizing facts in history. How learning really works is still a mystery. But your mind needs to flex itself with different exercises when you are young to prepare you to think in different ways throughout your life.

If you decided as you were growing up that you wanted to use only one arm, the muscles in the unused arm would wither, and every action that required two arms would be impossible for you. The same is true with the mind. If you don't use parts of it through different kinds of learning, then in the future, when you need these kinds of learning and thinking, you won't have them. Those parts of your mind will have withered.

Learning is a much-needed skill. Education teaches you *how to learn,* probably the most important mental skill a person can have. Life is an experience that requires continual learning: on the job, solving problems to get through the day, or working with new technology. When your mind has developed "muscle" through a good education, you can deal with new challenges — and life will give you many. As a learner, your life will be both productive and exciting.

So the next time you ask, *"Why do I have to take this course?"* remember the withered arm. You have to develop all the parts of your brain. When parts of it wither, you may never be able to enliven them. Career opportunities and life experiences will simply be beyond your grasp.

Work the material.

Processor-minded students know instinctively — or have discovered — that learning comes in layers. And layering takes time. For example, imagine getting a job where you have to learn 100 pieces of new information, information you have never heard of before. If you learn it quickly and well, you'll impress your boss. You want to do that because you know that's how people get pay raises and job promotions. What do you do? You learn by layering.

Learning information means coming back to it over and over again. But do you just keep reading the list over and over? That's the slow way. You know about learning, so you arrange the information in different ways. You make outlines or charts. You group different pieces of information by category, trying to see the whole picture these 100 items represent. If these pieces lend themselves to pictures, you draw pictures. Or you put each item on a card — word on one side, meaning on the other. It's like studying a foreign language, which is essentially what you're learning here: something foreign to you. You come back to your cards, charts, and drawings several times over several days. Because you've *worked with the material* instead of just memorizing a list, you understand it as a whole and as pieces. You're coming at the material from several angles and using repetition.

Think of it this way: If learning comes in layers, it's like making a fancy cake. Imagine a plain cake, no layers, no icing. This is just a lump of cake, a lump of knowledge, not very interesting, not very memorable. You'll probably forget eating this cake in about a week. What happens if you slice it horizontally through its middle, putting frosting between the two layers you've just made and on top? Now it's becoming a more appetizing cake. Slice it into several layers, put a different flavor of frosting on each layer, and then put chocolate decorations on top. That's a cake you won't forget. So, too, with information. When you work the material, you make the information into an unforgettable academic cake.

Here's how it might work: Familiarize yourself with some ingredients of your academic cake before you get to class by reading the chapter or reviewing your notes. Listen to your teacher tell you how the ingredients go together and how to bake it. Go home and go over the recipe. Review what you've learned in class and fit it to what you already know to make sure you understand both parts. By the time you go to your next class and the teacher adds to your information, he or she makes the basic cake of knowledge more and more interesting. In later classes, you're adding layers, frosting them, and decorating the top. Now you can start really appreciating your cake. By the time the test comes around, you can celebrate this beautiful cake (your knowledge) and throw a party, making it memorable all the way!

You're in control.

Once you understand that learning is processing information, you might have to adjust your thinking. Your mind is not a container. It's a biological organism, a musical instrument, or a complex computer that constantly needs care and activity (thinking, learning) to stay healthy or well-maintained. When you process knowledge, organize it, and use it, you are *learning*. And what you learn will stay with you — because your mind will develop and grow along with the knowledge and information you absorb.

Be college smart. Most students who are frustrated by their grades get that way because they believe their minds are containers. They depend on the teacher to pour knowledge — facts, formulas, etc. — into their heads. What's more, these students expect the teacher to process that knowledge for them, much like what happened in grade school. Not so anymore. The learning responsibility is yours. The teacher uses class time to *present* information. Doing homework and studying are your ways of "processing" (understanding and retaining) knowledge. You'll want to read Andrea's story at the end of this chapter. She really struggled with this responsibility.

If you really learn the material, you get higher grades. If you don't put in the effort, you get lower grades. It's as simple as that. If your mind isn't in "receiving and processing mode," most knowledge just falls on the floor.

So decide right now. Is your mind a box or an engine, a jar or a machine? Are you going to wait around for someone to stuff bits of knowledge into the hole in your head (and hope you remember later where the bits are)? Or are you going to use your mind to absorb, organize, and process that knowledge? It takes time to do this, but it's the only way to develop the learning skills you need for college and, later, for life.

Once the students I worked with understood the difference between a mind that is a box and a mind that is a knowledge processor, they began telling me —

- *"It sounds dumb to say it now, but the fact that learning takes time each day and week was a new discovery for me."*

- *"Yes, I thought the teacher was supposed to "put" things in my head. When I began to think of my mind as a computer processor that I controlled, my grades went up immediately."*

- *"Whenever I start a new class, I say to myself, 'I'm going to get an A.' I can do it if I don't think about how hard the teacher is or how many books I have to read. I just focus on how I'm going to manage this new subject every day."*

- *"If I get an A in a course, I say to myself, 'I handled that. WOW! Good for me.' If I get a low grade, I say, 'I'm still acting like a kid in grade school.'"*

Listen to Dr. Bob —
Why you need to practice this Strategy for college

Earning high grades in college is much, much tougher than earning the same grades in high school. Much of your college work must be done independently, and college professors expect you to know how to learn on your own. Therefore, investing time and exerting effort become very important personal skills for the college learner. If you are used to getting most of your knowledge from teachers during class, and if you've come to rely pretty much on in-class reviews and in-class practice sessions to help you learn, you will be out of luck in college. Be college smart: Start NOW to practice learning on your own.

PSST! Turn on your mental processor. Now go back and "process" all those highlighted ideas.

Meet Andrea in the story that follows. This is the first in a number of student stories that will show you students in real situations. Some succeed because they use the Strategies; others get into trouble because they ignore the Strategies. These are not stories that happen occasionally. While we talk about Andrea as a single student, she and her story represent situations that occur with thousands of students in colleges across the country every day.

<u>Up close and personal</u>
Andrea and the problem of study groups

Andrea came to see me after a fairly disastrous first semester her freshman year. Her grade point average was poor, even though she had graduated with honors from a good high school.

As she and I talked, I discovered that Andrea didn't spend nearly enough time studying outside of class. I told her that she needed to put in more time learning the course material. If she continued to study only as much as she had in high school, she would jeopardize her standing in the college. She said that she understood.

Yet, at the end of the second semester, she came to see me again. Her grades were going to be just as bad this semester, and she wanted to know what was going to happen to her. She was afraid to go home for the summer to face her parents. I asked her what had gone wrong. Hadn't she put in more time on her studies? She was quick to assure me that she had spent hours and hours studying.

As I asked more questions, I discovered that Andrea added more "study" hours by joining several study groups — she didn't like the idea of spending time alone studying, so she and some of her friends thought that it would be more fun to study as a group. "Fun" was the key word here. She and her friends may have put in the time, but they hadn't gotten the results. Why? They didn't understand the concept of study: it's private, it's solitary, and it's work. They wanted it to be social, lively, and fun.

When Andrea wasn't studying with her "group," she was studying in her dorm room, where someone else was always watching TV, listening to music, or just hanging out.

By the end of her freshman year, Andrea was already at a crisis point. Her academic record would be submitted to the college's Academic Review Committee. I chaired this committee, so I could speak to her bluntly about her chances. If the committee allowed her to return for a probationary semester, to give her "one more chance," I wanted her to understand two things: why her study groups didn't work and what she needed to do to really study.

First, study groups take maturity and serious preparation. That's why juniors and seniors are better suited to studying in groups. Older students understand that they must come to a study group already knowing the material. They meet as "experts" to look at the material from different perspectives and exchange high-level insights, not to rehash obvious facts. It's like an academic scrimmage, where everybody plays at a "pro" level.

Second, study groups are short-term strategies. They meet before tests and final exams, acting as a sort of an ultimate review. They don't meet three times a week all semester just to talk about the course.

Third, members are chosen wisely, recognizing what each can contribute to the group. No vampires are allowed. Vampires are lazy, unprepared students who hope to come and "listen," to suck up the knowledge that the other members have worked hard to acquire.

I then asked Andrea if her study groups fit my description. She admitted that they did not. She and her friends just sat around and talked. They moaned about their papers and their home-work. They discussed other students in their class, what everyone did last weekend, and the latest gossip. The amount of time spent talking about the course material was minimal and superficial because they all came hoping to learn something from someone else. They were all vampires; their conversations were doomed to go nowhere. I was not surprised. This is a common problem, even among some upperclassmen.

As far as studying in her dorm room, even Andrea knew that was hopeless.

Why, I asked, had Andrea waited so long to see me? She had known all along that the semester wasn't going well. She now had created two disastrous semesters. She finally admitted that she'd come now only because she feared being dropped from the college. She came to see if she could have another chance so that she could tell her parents that things were not as bad as they seemed.

Her circumstances were actually every bit as bad as they seemed. The Academic Review Commit-tee might give her one more chance, but she was very likely to waste it if she didn't come to terms with the concept of study. She would have to learn how to hit the books hard — something she had never done before. She had to figure out how to process information, not just do the assigned readings and occasional homework.

And, lastly, she was going to have to learn how to teach herself and not rely on the instructor to tell her what she had to know. Andrea looked at me blankly. What did I mean by "teach herself"? She usually did the assigned readings. She and I talked about different teaching and learning styles and how they should change over the years.

I told her about my son's fourth-grade experience in math. The fourth-grade teacher had practiced the multiplication tables every day. Over and over, the students played a game until they had all learned all their math facts: from one times one to twelve times twelve. The teacher used repetition in the classroom to help the students learn.

With grade school experiences like these, many students get the idea that this is what teachers are supposed to do — use class time as learning time. These students misunderstand that such a grade-school approach existed to help *very young students*. A decade later, Andrea still expected the teacher to teach Andrea what she needed to know during class time.

That's not how college (or high school, for that matter) is supposed to work. The teacher no longer practices with students in class. Andrea was supposed to use her time outside of class to practice on her own. She had to organize what she needed to learn. Then she had to figure out how to learn it, using repetition, lists, charts, notes — whatever it took to get the job done. (Remember the earlier section on **Independence and Control**?)

Andrea squirmed at this new idea. She had never thought about her predicament like this before. This sounded hard. It sounded like too much responsibility. She wanted to know if this was fair. Wasn't the teacher paid to teach? In college and in high school, too, the teacher is an expert who presents information. The students, however, must do the learning.

What happened to Andrea? Unfortunately, she dropped out of college. She sent me a note saying she got a job and hoped to return to college "soon."

Dean's commentary

Andrea was just not ready for college work. I'm sure she knew earlier in the semester that the study groups weren't working, but she didn't want to face it. She wanted to be with friends more than she wanted to be alone with her notes and her books.

Andrea is like so many students who think that they can approach college work just as they handled high school. She could study a little bit here and there, pay attention in class, and hand in assignments. She thought that would do it. No, it won't. College is not high school away from home.

College is harder, and to make it harder still, you spend less time in the classroom than you did in high school. For example, your math class meets every day in high school. In college, your math class will probably meet only three times a week. Yet the pace at which you move through the textbook will accelerate tremendously. Think about it: shorter semesters, fewer class meetings, harder material, a faster pace. That means more studying — more "processing" on your own outside of class. While you can't measure the difference exactly, you'll be asked to learn twice the material in half the time. As an older student, you're supposed to handle that.

Studying — absorbing information and then relating it to other information you've already absorbed — takes concentration, quiet, and privacy. It's work that has to be done without distraction, giving your subject full attention and whatever time it takes to finish.

Andrea didn't like hearing that college was so much work. Where was the fun? That's another major point she was missing: If she could learn to study with some efficiency, she'd have more time to be with her friends. (More on that later.) **RU READY?**

Strategy 2

Your study place —
space, quiet, and comfort: your body prefers them, and your mind needs them

This is your personal place, where you finish up one day of learning and plan for the next. A good study space is well-equipped and helps you think. After all, the more productive you are in your study place, the more time you will have in your day to do all of those other things you've listed on your Weekly Activity Map. A good study place is a valuable tool you use to manage your time, control your days, and learn.

Learn about yourself

Check all that apply.

When I study at home —

_____ I like to sprawl out on my bed or the floor.

_____ I study wherever I can: the kitchen, my room, the family room, etc.

_____ I study in different places every day for variety.

_____ I study in my bedroom because that's where my music and my computer are.

_____ I like to study near a television because I like the distraction.

_____ My study area is private, quiet, and comfortable.

_____ I don't answer phone calls.

_____ My study area is respected by my entire family.

If you're *really* going to learn — retain knowledge, not cram — and get high grades, you have to study. The first step in developing good study habits is having a place at home to study. It should be a place of your own, a place that is quiet and comfortable, away from the noise and commotion of everyday life.

Do you study in other places? Of course you do. Just going to class each day, paying careful attention to the teacher, taking good notes, asking thoughtful questions, and actively participating in discussions is one form of studying. Study halls or study periods during your school days are also places and times to get in some studying. Even catching a few moments of study here and there can be significant because they can add up. But don't think of them as your basic study effort. The best and most learning you can do takes place at home in your own private study place.

Be college smart. This idea is important, and so it's worth repeating. Study in a place that gives you the best results for the time you spend studying. After all, you want your studying to be efficient as well as successful. Remember: You're trying to take control of your days. To do that, you have to MANAGE your time and make it work for you.

Studying productively helps you fit into your day all the other important activities of your busy life — team practices, club meetings, music lessons, relaxing, and so forth. At the end of this chapter, you'll read about Kristen, who ran into trouble. Her study places were not productive. She thought she was studying, but she was really wasting her time, and she damaged her grades.

An efficient work space

You would not normally like to sleep on a hard floor, or eat while running, or watch a movie with people talking over the dialogue or blocking the screen. It's the same with learning. Your study place should be well-chosen, well-located, well-organized, and comfortable.

Having a particular study area, a place that you can call your own — where you can sit, concentrate, and learn — is crucial. In fact, a good study place can very well affect *how* and *if* you study well, both factors that determine your learning success.

Let's face it: Studying is work. It requires dedication, concentration, and routine. Once you begin to study each subject every day, you will develop a stronger interest in *all* your courses. They will become more enjoyable. It's true! Try it! To get the job done right, your study place should be well-designed for the work you will do there. In fact, efficiency is important to you because your study *time* should have an official beginning and end. You want to complete your work within a specific amount of time. (We'll be talking a lot more about study time in Strategies 7 and 8.)

A well-equipped study place

Organizing your study place actually prepares you to work in the adult world. All careers, professions, and jobs require that you manage your time efficiently in a fully equipped work area where you can get things done. It could be an office, a workstation, a laboratory, or even a fully loaded laptop computer that travels with you from place to place.

Similarly, the quality and efficiency of your study place is directly connected to your ability to learn and to earn good grades. Most of the time, studying requires a desk or table with a large enough work surface for you to spread out and have everything at hand that you need. What do you need? Textbooks, notebooks, writing utensils, calculator, dictionary and thesaurus, and a good reading lamp. When you're doing a "first read" of some class materials, like a novel, you can be sitting in a relaxing chair. But generally, when you read and reread material, you need to make notes and outlines, so you have to be at your desk.

While I know a lot of students like to study while flopped on their beds, it's not a good idea. A large part of studying involves organizing course materials and class notes as well as doing homework assignments — which means writing things down. Being slouched on a bed makes writing difficult. (It's hard to find a comfortable writing position, and later, you'll have an equally hard time trying to read your ragged handwriting.)

And if for no other reason, don't study in bed because it confuses your body and your mind. A bed signals your body to relax, not concentrate.

How good is your current study place? Here's a checklist for you:

_____ A quiet place, away from the activities in the house.

_____ A BIG ENOUGH desk or table.

_____ A bright desk lamp.

_____ A place to keep a set of learning tools
(*calculators, highlighters, index cards, scissors, stapler, etc.*).

_____ Reference books: dictionaries, grammar guide, thesaurus, etc.

_____ A good desk chair. Your body, as well as your mind, has to adopt the right
attitude — one that means business.

An undisturbed location

Just as your body likes to do things at certain times, like eating and sleeping, your mind likes the familiarity of the same place. Arrange your study place to suit the work you are doing: learning. That means not only must the place you choose be well-equipped, it must also be a place free of distractions — no people walking by, no televisions in the background, and no family conversations within earshot. Sisters and brothers, even mothers and fathers, must respect and stay out of your study place. In a few pages, you'll read about Ethan, who couldn't work because of his roommate and the noise in his dorm room.

Put on your study cap.

Have you heard of die-hard, passionate sports fans who have their "game clothes"? These dedicated fans do anything to show their loyalty and to bring good luck to their favorite team by wearing team shirts, pants, costumes, and weird headgear, like wedges of cheese or antlers. Frequently, they've had these clothes for years, and the rips and holes are obvious — all the better to show their devotion.

Believe it or not, I've known students in college who act the same way to show their loyalty and devotion to their studies. Not only do they have their particular study place, they have their study clothes. These are their most comfortable "threads" because comfort is a good studier's goal. You want comfort in body as well as in mind. *"When I wear these clothes, I can learn anything,"* said one student.

And besides comfort, clothes can be a signal. They warn other people who might drop by a study area or pass by a table in the library. *"When I'm wearing my red cap, stay away. I'm studying and don't want to be disturbed unless the building is on fire,"* says another student.

Some students can waste many hours after school *trying* to study and do homework! They don't get much done. They are studying in a noisy place where they can't concentrate. They frequently interrupt their study time by getting involved with family members. They're on the phone with friends, answering it whenever it rings, or they've got one eye on the TV. (One student told me that he got plenty of studying done — "during commercials.") Many students listen to music while they study. But the fact is that students who don't study in a quiet, isolated place feel that their studying is never done. They don't have a sense of start and finish. The hours and the distractions just keep going on. Their studying either drags on or never starts in the first place.

As a high school student, setting up a study place can be easy, especially if you have your own room at home. The danger of being in your own room, however, is that it might have a television, a computer with games and email, a music system, etc. If these temptations are difficult for you to resist (and they can be), pull the plug on them while you study. Or ask your parents if you can set up a study place in some other area of your home, away from noise, as well as temptations. Once your parents understand that you're serious and you don't want to be interrupted, they will help you protect your time and space. They'll record your favorite programs for you so you can watch them later. They'll keep your brothers and sisters out of your study area. Most parents will do just about anything to help you.

Speaking of parents, if you need to find a study place that's not your own room, you will probably have to ask for their help in setting up the area. If there are other students in your family, parents may have to help work out a plan for everyone who needs a study place.

Privacy equals productivity.

The modern cell phone is really a wonder of digital technology. TV commercials promise that if you don't have one, you're pitifully out of touch. And, of course, the cell phone is no longer just a talking device. It's a notebook, a photo album, a musical library, and a way of passing notes to your friends (just like in grade school).

But when you're trying to study, the cell phone becomes a tremendous distraction. Leaving your cell phone on — so it rings whenever your many friends feel like talking — interrupts your concentration. The result? Either studying will take much longer than it should, or these distractions can prevent you from learning much at all.

So whenever you say to yourself, *"I'm being a student now,"* turn off the phone and put it in your backpack. Turn off your email program, too, so you can't hear it tunefully announce every new message that lands in your inbox. In fact, turn off all the digital devices that you use to "stay connected." You'll get more done in less time. When you study, you have to take a break from your social life. When you've finished studying, you can return all those calls in your voicemail box and sort through your email messages. No, you're not cutting yourself off from your friends; you're only separating yourself from them for a little while.

About music in the background

To understand what you are reading, to make sure you're not missing steps in a math problem, to memorize definitions or science formulas, or to write the draft of an essay *requires concentration and focus.* Hearing the words to familiar songs in the background will distract you. Your mind wants to sing along. Even music with a regular beat distracts; you may find your head bobbing to the beat or your fingers or foot tapping it out. Beats are hard to resist. For these reasons, doing mental tasks takes longer with music.

Most students find that they do their best studying in a perfectly quiet place. But if you find you need background sound, play some music that pleases the ear without distracting your mind. Try meditation music — there's plenty of it out there that provides a kind of nondistracting, relaxing sound. But be moderate in your need for background sounds. Recognize that most studying demands absolute quiet.

Why? Because if you stop to think about it, there are different intensities of study. Some study is easier, like making homemade flash cards to memorize terms. Other study, like working on difficult math problems or writing the first draft of an essay, is much harder and may need absolute silence. Listen to your mind. If you're having a hard time getting the job done, turn off the music — no matter how relaxing it seems — and try studying in quiet.

And as much as music distracts, using the TV as "background noise" makes studying nearly impossible. Your attention is completely divided. You spend a good part of your energy trying to tune out dialogue and loud commercials so you can hear your own thoughts. You can't "sort of" listen to the TV (with an occasional glance at the screen) *and* concentrate on your studies. Plus, studying during the commercials of your favorite program is not going to work, either. You can't do high-level thinking in five-minute pieces in between scenes. Instead, record all your favorite programs, and watch them later when you have time — you'll *save* time because you won't have to sit through the commercials.

Portable quiet

If finding quiet in your house is difficult, you might want to invest in a pair of soft earplugs. They become "portable quiet" devices: Keep them handy in your room to use whenever the general commotion of home life is just too distracting. As a college student, you might find that earplugs are your answer to a good night's sleep in a chaotic dorm.

Earplugs can be found at drugstores, discount stores, and even hardware stores. A pair costs about as much as a soft drink, well worth the price.

Get it together.

You can be the most organized, the most serious, and the most determined student in the world. But if you do not have a good study place, all those wonderful qualities become practically meaningless.

When you are studying and learning, the "DO NOT DISTURB" sign should be hanging in a place for everyone to see. When you have your own private and personal study place, you can control the quality and quantity of studying that you know you need. Studying and learning are your responsibility. When you take the time to create a place all your own, you accomplish great academic things, the kind of things anyone would expect from a college smart person like you.

Listen to Dr. Bob —

Why you need to practice this Strategy for college

Remember what we said in this section of the last Strategy? Unlike high school, most learning in college is done OUTSIDE of class. For each hour a college student spends in class, he or she is expected to study *two to three hours outside of class.* That's why college gives you all of that unscheduled time. Your instructors expect you to use a good portion of it to study. Knowing how to study efficiently is an important skill. However, even if you have great study skills, you *still must have a productive place* to study in order to get your work done.

Start learning the value of a good study place now! By the time you get to college, you'll already know what working in a productive study place feels like. That means you'll be smart enough to abandon the noisy dorm and find a place on campus where you can really get something done. The places are there on campus, and you'll find a good one because you'll know what to look for.

Choosing and using a good study place right now means that you're taking a major step toward personal success in high school and later in college. Remember that getting into college is only the first step. *Graduating from college is the real goal.* A good study place is one of the essential Strategies that will help you get that college diploma on time!

PSST! Now go back to the **Learn about yourself** that began this Strategy and compare your answers to what you see in the highlighted sections. Do you need to work on your study place? That's okay. It's a step in the right direction. Every time you use a Strategy, you are helping yourself and becoming more and more college smart!

Up close and personal

Kristen and the problem of privacy

Kristen was a pretty good student in high school, but her grades suddenly fell dramatically in college. She came to see me about a scheduling matter, and when I saw her grades, I began asking her questions about her study habits. She told me that early in grade school, she always did her homework at the kitchen table before dinner, so her mom could help her. Kristen continued this habit up until high school, with her little brothers coming and going as they watched after-school programs in the next room.

In high school, she found that working at the kitchen table was too distracting because her homework was becoming harder. So she moved to the quiet of her bedroom. (Quiet? Afraid not.) Kristen had a phone, a computer connected to the Internet, and an email account. Although Kristen didn't realize it, she was really trading one set of distractions for another. The noise of a couple of brothers and sisters was replaced by the calls and messages of 10 friends who always "urgently" needed her attention. She told me that she spent a very long time getting her homework done in high school, but she thought it was because her teachers had piled on so much work!

In her first semester at college, Kristen tried to study in the dorm and barely got by. Her grades were much lower than in high school. At the start of the second semester, she moved to a study lounge in the dorm, which really turned out to be a more of a social place for students to meet and talk. Her grades weren't getting any better, so next she tried the library. I asked her to describe her study place in the library, and she told me she studied at a table near the stairwell where her friends could see her and stop to say hello.

What was wrong? Kristen thought she studied a lot. She put in the time but she could never quite accept that a good portion of study must be done in a private and quiet place. She needed to find a small, comfortable study place in a back corner of the library, in a non-traffic area where she could find the quiet to concentrate.

Some light study can succeed with movement and talk going on around you, but for you to learn in-depth and to keep the knowledge long-term, most study requires quiet and privacy. At first, Kristen couldn't stand being cut off from the activities around her. Her grades didn't improve until she discovered that she had to hit the books hard *in private* and then use other time to socialize.

It wasn't until her junior year (halfway through college) that Kristen got used to studying in a quiet, private place. She told me that her problem was almost like being afraid to be alone. Until college, she had always liked studying in places where people were around her or in contact with her. That's what her mind expected when she sat down to study. The problem was that her mind couldn't learn efficiently with the distractions, so she always took forever to get things done. In college, with so much more studying to do, she couldn't keep up. Fortunately, she was determined, and she finally graduated, earning very good grades in her last semesters. Her final comment to me was this: *"Until college, I had developed a really bad habit about where to study. I'd have saved myself a lot of trouble if I had developed a habit of working in quiet places early on."*

Up close and personal
Ethan and his roommate: different lifestyles

Ethan was frustrated. His roommate, Paul, returned to their room every night after dinner and watched TV in their cramped quarters. Ethan found he couldn't tune out the sound no matter how hard he tried. He wasn't getting anything done in what he considered one of his "prime" blocks of study time. Each night, by the time Paul finished with his TV programs, Ethan had lost his edge — it was too late, and he wasn't sharp enough to put in late hours studying. What's more, he had an 8:00 a.m. German class four days a week.

At first, Ethan asked Paul to use headphones, but Paul couldn't find them and never seemed to get around to buying a new pair. Other kids began stopping in to watch TV with Paul, and Ethan felt like he didn't have control over his own room.

He was right. He didn't. He needed to get out of that room, or he wasn't going to get anything done. Ethan was in a situation that seriously affects many college students: roommates who blare music, play video games, or turn the room into the dorm floor's social center. I told Ethan that the best thing he could do for himself was to pack his notes and his books and find himself a study place where he could go every night.

Any college or university that is serious about academics provides places for individual study: quiet study lounges in dorms or the union, study carrels (like work cubes or rooms) in the library.

Some schools provide study floors, special floors within the dorm that attract students who want to live in a noise-restricted area. The students who sign up for these living arrangements are usually those who are more serious about college. Noise-restricted dorm floors enforce the rules: no loud music, no noisy gatherings, and respect for the study atmosphere. The students who live on these floors all take learning seriously. They leave the dorm and go to places like the recreation center to let off steam. I suggested to Ethan that he might want to consider signing up for a study floor for his sophomore year.

Right now, however, he needed a plan to work around his roommate. I told Ethan to start looking for a quality study area. On our campus, there were several study havens, like the Science Library in the Dental School and areas in the Student Union. Some students had found great success using the cafeterias during off hours. The many cafeterias were quiet and had big tables.

The trick for Ethan was to find a place with like-minded students — students who may sit near him but who would respect his privacy and maintain a quiet area. I gave Ethan a few more places to check out and asked him to come back in two weeks to let me know how he was doing.

Two weeks later, Ethan was back and reporting great success. He had discovered three study places. Two he used during his afternoon study sessions between classes, and one place he went to every night. Not only was he getting his studying done, but he was getting to bed at a decent hour because he was studying more efficiently.

Ethan told me that when he arrived at his study places, he would see the same students sitting in the same chairs within these areas. They were all used to each other being there — in fact, he'd grown to expect to see his fellow students — but each respected the other's privacy. *"It's like being in a group, but not being in a group. It's sort of weird, but it works. We all know why we're there, and we leave each other alone."* This group of students recognized the value of a quiet place where they could concentrate and be productive.

Each night, Ethan returned to his room no later than 10:30 or 11:00 p.m. He'd put in earplugs if his roommate was still watching TV, pull the pillow over his head, and get enough sleep so that he was fresh and alert in his German class. He had been half asleep in that class for weeks because he was staying up too late trying to get his work done.

Another big advantage for Ethan was that he now had time to join a basketball club. He hadn't had time for basketball before, and he had resented it. Now, however, he was studying so much more efficiently that he had time and energy for intramurals and extracurricular activities — he'd joined the digital-photography club! He felt in control of his life. Once he got his study places straightened out, everything else fell into place: sleep, study, courses, and social time.

Dean's commentary

Andrea (from Strategy 1) and Ethan were on opposite sides of the study problem. Andrea didn't want to be alone to study in peace and quiet. Ethan wanted just that situation but was frustrated because Paul, his roommate, wouldn't cooperate.

Furthermore, Ethan discovered what Andrea couldn't figure out: When you get your studying done efficiently — when you have the peace and quiet to be productive — you have less stress and more time to do other things. You have more time for fun and more time to be social, and you get the sleep you need to stay healthy. You feel better about yourself and about life. Oh, yes, and don't forget this: Your grades are great, and you don't lose your career dreams. Andrea lost hers. Ethan did not.

College gives you the freedom to choose. How you use that freedom makes all the difference. You can act like Andrea, like Paul, or like Ethan.

Right now, if you were given the choice of starting a research paper that's due in a couple of weeks or watching TV, which would you choose? In grade school you weren't expected to be able to manage time or use your willpower to get things done. By high school, you should be developing those powers, so you can use the freedom you'll be given in college. How are you doing? Where, when, and how well you study are ways you exercise your freedom to choose. **RU READY?**

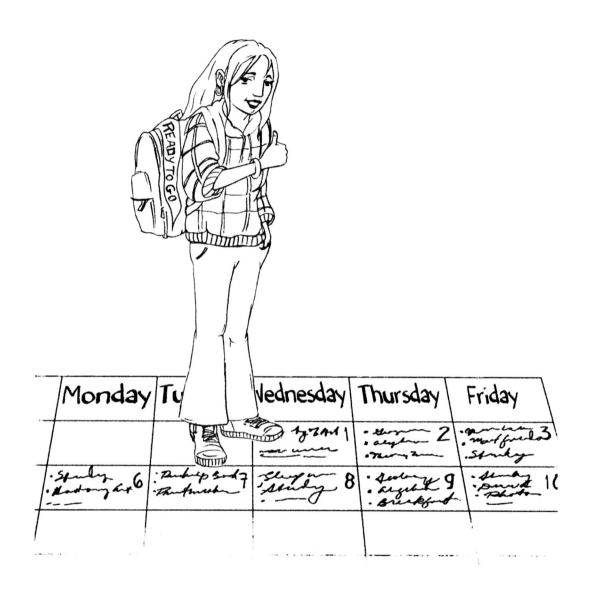

Strategy 3

The first two weeks —
what you should do while everyone else is trying to find a good seat

The semester is beginning. Maybe it's even a new year getting started. You've got fresh notebooks and maybe some new teachers and a new class schedule. This is when controlling your courses starts, and organization is the name of the game. Are you ready? Let's go!

Learn about yourself

When a new semester begins, what should you do to start it off right? To get you thinking, assign each statement below a number from 1 to 5 according to how important it is to you. The most important actions will get 5s. The least important actions will get 1s.

_____ Make a notebook for each course.

_____ Introduce yourself to each new teacher.

_____ Talk to other students to find out if your new courses or teachers are hard or easy.

_____ Look through all your textbooks.

_____ Make a daily study schedule.

_____ Look over course outlines and paying attention to grading policies, tests, major assignments, and important due dates.

_____ Find a good seat near your friends before the teacher creates a seating chart.

_____ See your guidance counselor to review your previous semester.

In your opinion, why is it hard to earn a high grade in any course? Again, score these answers 1 to 5 (5s for the items that you consider most difficult; 1s for the least difficult).

_____ Difficult tests.

_____ Difficult teacher.

_____ The subject is difficult for you.

_____ Too many other things to do this semester.

_____ Too many other difficult courses.

_____ The competition from other students is too tough.

_____ The subject is not interesting.

Starting fresh

Every new semester is a new beginning. If this new semester starts a whole new year, your courses, your teachers, your class schedule, and many other things are new. And if last year seems "years away," that's okay — because it means a lot has changed in your life. You should hope that a lot has changed in your academic life, too.

Every new semester gives you new opportunities. A new semester means you are moving one more level up that learning mountain. Courses are getting harder, and the demands on you as a student are greater. Or they should be. If they are not, something's wrong. Even if a new semester means mostly the same courses with the same teachers — and even if you have an *A* average — you still need to set new, higher goals for yourself. Starting a new semester with new plans for better things is the best way to develop as a student and control your education.

What should you do to start a new school term? Before you step into that first class, you should completely review the last semester, preferably with your counselor. These are the items you should cover:

- What grades did you earn last semester?
- Were you satisfied with them?
- Could your grades have been higher?
- Were they consistently high, or were they irregular?
- If you got lower grades than the semester before, do you know why?
- Did you really learn the course material or did you cram a lot and work just for grades?
- What do you want to change in this new semester? How do you plan to make those changes?

For your review to work for you, you have to answer these questions honestly.

How to look at the first two weeks

At the start of each new semester, most students don't do a lot of planning, thinking, or organizing. If it's the start of a new year, they get caught up in a flurry of other activities. They renew acquaintances. They decorate their lockers. They jockey for a seat near their friends in each class. They sort through the social groups formed by different classes. They sign up for extracurricular activities. In all the excitement, it's hard to concentrate on courses.

Most students don't get down to business right away. Before they know it, they find themselves facing the first tests in each class. The early weeks *have just disappeared*. Where did the time go?

Semester after semester, students are caught off guard by first tests. Yet despite this all-too-familiar pattern, do many students worry about the time warp that seems to put them "behind" even before first tests and first assignments are due? Amazingly, few do. Many will say, *"Nothing much really happens in any course in the first two to four weeks."* Others say, *"I don't really know how much I need to study until I start getting grades back. If I start getting low grades, I'll try to study more. If my grades are 'high enough,' I know I'm all right doing what I'm doing."*

 Be college smart. As important as the end of a semester is, the best students I've known tell me that they concentrate on the *first* two weeks. Getting off to a strong start makes their courses easier and earns these students the highest grades, even in courses they dislike. Generally speaking, students who use their time during the first two weeks of a course to think and plan do the best at the end.

Here's a real-world example: Have you ever heard anyone say, *"That team lost the game in the first ten minutes"?* What does that mean? Usually two things: The team did not come to the game in shape or ready to play. And the team did not size up the opposition very well. So what should you do the first two weeks of the semester? Come to the classroom ready to study on the very first day. And size up the course.

Sizing up the course is easy. At the beginning of any semester, the teacher spends time talking about the course, course materials — like texts — and what he or she expects of students. The teacher also goes through a course outline to let you know when major assignments are due and when tests are scheduled, along with how much each counts toward your final grade. Pay attention to this information. The course outline gives you an overview of the semester and describes the amount of work involved in the course. As you'll learn later, this information gives you the power to control the course.

Remember the Clueless and Typical Students? They don't listen to any of this very well because *they've heard it all before.* The College Smart Student listens for two things in particular: how much material will be covered during the semester and what the teacher expects students to do. The College Smart Student is out there working, and working ahead, even as other students are waiting around for something to happen. There's plenty happening. The Clueless and Typical Students are just not aware that the semester has begun to roll without them.

Where your stress *really* comes from

Lots of students spend the first two weeks taking it easy. Many think they are saving their energy for when things "really get going," late in the semester. What they don't realize is that their slow start to the semester actually *increases* their stress later on. Because they don't start on the first day, they seem always to be playing "catch up" in their classes. They think that's the way a semester is supposed to work. In fact, the way to decrease your stress is to get a head start on the semester. Be focused, energetic, and active during the first two weeks.

Some college students who learn this lesson find that getting the right start improves their grades and their life so much that they become almost fanatical about how they handle the first two weeks. They spend as much time studying during these early weeks as most students usually spend on the last two weeks of the semester. (It's a very good idea.) They cut everything out of their daily schedule that isn't essential — especially hanging out with friends who waste lots of time during the first two weeks.

What should you do? While you don't have to go to the extreme of entirely cutting yourself off from your friends, you should start the semester off with a bang. Getting off to a good start means creating a *head start* for yourself. If you do, you'll never feel rushed again. Your grades will go up and stay up. It's hearing the starting gun that will give you a head start. Use the 7 steps described in this Strategy, and after two weeks, you'll have a real advantage — you'll do better with less stress, all semester long.

Starting the semester smart

When you get off to a strong start in the first two weeks of the semester, you are much like the team that "comes ready to play." You are getting yourself in shape and sizing up your courses. Here are seven basic steps that will get you ready "to play" at the start of a new semester. Make sure you do each one!

1. Evaluate your success last semester. Most students walk out of final exams and close the door on those courses. With a sigh of relief, students say to themselves, *"That's over."* They don't have to think about those subjects anymore. Right? Wrong. If you're really on top of it, you'll learn something about yourself from each course. What did you do that helped you succeed in the course? What did you do that hurt your success? Remind yourself of what worked and try to build on that strategy in the future. Recall what you did that clouded your understanding, put you behind, or cost you points on a test. Resolve that you won't make those same mistakes next semester.

List your good habits

What kinds of good habits are you looking for? Here are a few examples. Add your own on the blank lines.

Following a weekly study schedule.

Recopying your textbook and class notes each night, reviewing them, highlighting important points, and adding comments.

Completing assignments carefully and on time.

Rereading each chapter to improve your understanding of the material.

Doing more math or science problems than your teacher assigns.

Talking to your teachers after tests are returned to see how you could have improved your grade.

Making lists or flashcards of things that have to be memorized.

Creating outlines or charts to summarize course material.

Keeping a calendar of tests and due dates and working ahead.

_____

_____

_____

_____

_____

List your bad habits

What kind of bad habits got in the way of your success? Here are a few common problems that students wrestle with. Think of any bad habits that you have and write them on the blanks.

Studying irregularly or haphazardly.

Putting off assignments until the last minute.

Taking poor class notes.

Coming to class unprepared.

Not paying attention in class.

Cramming for tests at the last minute.

Not writing enough drafts of papers.

Not rereading course material.

Missing deadlines and being penalized.

Not asking questions to clarify assignments early on.

Not talking to teachers about your progress.

_____

_____

_____

_____

_____

Now make a chart of your good and bad habits. Put it in your daily planner or tape it to the inside cover of your subject notebooks. Read it often. Use the information you discovered about yourself to remind you what you should and shouldn't be doing to succeed this semester.

One more thing: If you are surprised or puzzled because any of last semester's final grades were lower than you expected, schedule a conference with that teacher. Talk about how you did on the final exam, and if you had problems, ask for advice on improving the way you study for that subject. Even if you'll never have that instructor or subject again, you'll learn something that you can apply to other courses.

But remember this very important point: Talking to a teacher about grades is NOT a complaining session. Teachers don't give low grades because they don't like you or because they're having a bad day. When it comes to grades, teachers have two main goals: to be accurate and to be consistent. *Focus on your purpose: You're going to the teacher to learn what you did wrong and try to improve, not to argue a grade.*

2. Take some time early in the first week to slowly page through all the books, manuals, and materials that are used in the course. Don't wait until you're told to use a particular book before you open it. Look over all the course materials. Be familiar with the whole package from the start. It's like planning a trip. You want to know where you're going and how you're going to get there — and how to prevent unpleasant surprises along the way. You do that by learning as much as you can about your "journey" even before you start traveling.

3. Read and reread all the information a teacher hands out at the beginning of the semester. These course outlines, directions, summaries, and grading policies are your teacher's way of emphasizing what the course will be about and how it will be organized. This written material is your first opportunity to "tune in" to the teacher's "academic station." Highlight or underline the important points. File these pages somewhere safe so you can go back to them anytime throughout the semester. Review this information often. It will keep you focused and in control of the course. You'll always know what's going on and what's coming up.

If you have questions on any of these all-important details, *see the teacher right away.*

4. Use a monthly calendar to map out what's going on in all your courses. Buy a monthly planner in an office-supply store. Some are designed just for students. The important thing here is to see the entire month in one glance.

Using your course outlines, jot down dates in your planner for all tests and major assignments for each month in the semester. Once you've entered this information, your calendar gives you a bird's-eye view of every month. You now have a master calendar, showing you what's going on in ALL your courses.

Because your calendar gives you an overview of the *whole month*, it alerts you to weeks with heavy loads and warns you when tests and assignments are just around the corner. You now have the advantage of looking ahead. Students who don't know one week what's going on next week always get into trouble. They fool themselves into thinking that there's not much to do this week *because they don't know what's due next week!* Keep on top of your courses by always knowing what's coming up.

You can update your calendar if your teacher adds more important "events" as the semester progresses. Choose a planner with dates that have lines to write on so you can fit several items on each day. Some days may be busier than others.

5. Before two weeks have gone by, have one private conversation with the teacher. You have to get over the idea that talking to teachers is "uncool" or a manipulative way to get higher grades. Students who consistently earn *A*s tell me that talking privately with teachers gives them a better comfort level in all classes, even with the hardest teachers. Why? Talking to each teacher privately, face to face, makes students feel more at ease. The teacher is no longer so distant. You can say things privately to a teacher that you would not say in class. By sharing information about yourself, you turn the teacher into exactly what he or she should be: a person interested in your success, your academic ally who will help you learn and succeed in a subject. The teacher is not your opponent.

True, not all teachers are easy to talk to. However, most enjoy talking to students outside of class. Here are some possible topics:

1. Talk to the teacher about what interests you in this course.

2. Let the teacher know if this is a new subject for you.

3. Tell the teacher if you are finding the course difficult.

4. Ask about tips on how to study or how much time the teacher expects you to spend on the subject each night or each week.

5. Do you like this subject enough to study it in college? If so, ask the teacher what kind of courses you would take if you majored in it. And, as a college graduate, what careers would be open to you?

6. Ask how the subject relates to "real life," or how you'll use this information later on.

7. Have you noticed that this subject ties in with other courses you are taking? Talk to the teacher about how the content of the two courses fits together.

Then, if you should find yourself slipping in the course, or even getting a low grade on a test, talking to a teacher you already know on a personal level is easier than talking with a teacher you've never spoken to before. (You'll find more about talking to teachers in Strategy 5.)

6. Schedule a time to see your assigned counselor. Your high school counselor is your personal academic guide. Stay in touch with your counselor throughout the semester. A counselor can help you out of difficult situations, far more than you know. Consult your counselor regularly. (Three times a semester if you're doing well. Once a month if you're having problems.) What do you talk about? You should discuss the results of your own personal evaluation of last semester. Maybe your counselor can give you additional insights. Talk about your courses for this semester and the courses in which you feel weak or strong. Unlike teachers, who will talk about how to study for a particular course, counselors will give you general advice, an overview of different approaches to studying all your courses.

Decide how many times you should see your counselor. After your first meeting, schedule other appointments for the rest of the semester. Use them to talk about your progress in your courses and perhaps do some pre-college planning. To stay focused on your future, talk about your goals for college and for a career. Reporting regularly to your counselor keeps you on track. (More about this in Strategy 6.)

7. Make a chart for your grades. Yes, each teacher has your grades in a grade book, but the idea here is for you to track your progress and know your grades week by week. Just because you got an *A* on that last test, you shouldn't feel you can slack off, especially if your three earlier grades were lower. Tracking your grades lets you know where you really stand. (More on this in Strategy 10.)

Need help? Don't delay.

You're driving along in your car. It starts to make a bad sound, so you pull over and call a road service. You know you're in trouble and need expert help.

The same is true in school. You begin a new course, and within a few days, you're dragging behind the class. Or you begin a new section in a course, and suddenly, you're really confused. Or maybe it's the start of a new semester, and you quickly know that you don't have all your courses under control. In this case, and many others, you need expert help.

Your education, like a car with smoke pouring out of its hood, could use the services of an expert. Find one and get some help. Don't hesitate, and don't be embarrassed — you'll avoid some horrible situations.

Where do you start? Go to your teacher and your guidance counselor. They are ready to help you, and the more willing you are to take their advice, the quicker you will solve any problems.

Whether it is consulting your teachers privately or scheduling appointments with your counselor, DO IT. Be smart enough to get out in front of your problems early while they still can be solved. Learning how and when to get help is a skill that will come in handy in college, where things get harder still. Soon it will become as simple as changing a tire!

What about you?

Return to the section that began this Strategy, the section that asks you why you think it's hard to get high grades in your courses. See if you know better now how to handle each difficulty.

Difficult tests. Your one-page calendar will help you see when tests and assignments are due. Start studying early and mark your calendar to remind yourself of when to begin preparing for them. For example, if you're all jammed up with papers and assignments in Week Four, you'd better use time in the first three weeks to study for that "big" history test coming up in Week Five. Otherwise, you'll be overwhelmed. Here's the larger point: *It's time to change your thinking.* True, your calendar keeps you aware of assignment dates and test dates in your courses. But if you think of every day, every class, and every time you sit down to study as *preparing for your next test,* there's no need to scramble at the last minute to prep for a test.

Difficult teacher. Once you've established a personal connection with a teacher, asking even the most difficult teacher to help you through the rough spots of a course will be easier. Know what? He or she will do it! Teachers respect students who plan ahead and ask for help and advice.

Subject is difficult for you. Attack hard subjects with energy at the outset, particularly the first two weeks. Use your course outline to read ahead each day so you are always prepared for class. You'll already know something about what the teacher is introducing. Bring questions to your teacher, either in class or privately. Pay attention to how long it takes to prepare for this subject so you can allow enough time in your day for it. Doing all these things will help you get ahead early in the semester and will keep you moving at the teacher's pace. Once you're behind in a difficult subject, you're in serious trouble. Stay ahead, and you stay on top!

Too many other things to do. If you spend the first few days of the semester listening to what is expected of you in each course, you will have a better sense of how to pace yourself with non-academic activities throughout the semester. You'll be less likely to over-schedule your time.

Too many other difficult courses. If you jump-start *all* your courses, you will lessen the difficulty of each and do better in all.

The competition is too tough. However stiff the competition from other students, getting serious from the first day gives you the competitive edge over all those guys sitting around waiting for something to happen. Use the 7 tactics in this Strategy and adjust your thinking. Remember: Like the team that wins the game in the first ten minutes, *you've come to play.*

Managing the critical first two weeks is the way to get the upper hand in all your courses. With the right start, you'll control the semester. It won't control you. You'll get better grades, and the semester won't be so stressful or frustrating.

Listen to Dr. Bob —

Why you need to practice this Strategy for college

In college, there's no dead time at the beginning of the semester, no get-acquainted classes, no review of what the teacher hopes you already know. The semester starts on DAY ONE and moves at a pace that is very much faster than high school. I never grow tired of reminding students that college courses cover much more material than high school courses during the same or shorter period of time. In high school, you may spend five weeks studying a novel. Your college English professor will cover that novel in about a week, maybe two — that's three to six classes. Will you be ready for that pace?

You have to learn to start strong, or you'll be hopelessly behind from the very start. Follow the steps in this Strategy to get yourself and your courses organized. Review your performance last semester and learn from it. Get off to a strong start by familiarizing yourself with the materials in all your courses, and complete your calendar to anticipate the work that lies ahead. Start studying *right away* so you do well on first tests. (Don't get into the bad habit of relying on extra credit to boost low test grades. There's no extra credit in college.) Meet with your teachers, and schedule an appointment with your guidance counselor. Start tracking your grades as soon as you begin getting them, so you know where you stand. There's plenty to do in those first two weeks! And now you know it.

PSST! Now that you know how to think about the first two weeks, review the highlights to get those 7 steps in your head. You may not be reading this Strategy at the start of the semester, but you'll want to be mentally prepared when the next semester begins. (You can do steps 1, 4, 5, and 6 no matter where you are in the semester.)

MEETING IN SESSION

Up close and personal

Chad: Oui, oui! This is French — new courses always take more time.

Chad had two years of Spanish in high school, but he was tired of Spanish and wanted to take a new language to fulfill his college foreign-language requirement. Chad chose French. His girlfriend in high school had taken French, and she had liked it. Besides, Chad thought it might be cool to be able to go to restaurants and order wine with a French accent.

Day One in French 001: Chad finds himself a seat in the back of the room, and the instructor comes in speaking to the class in French. Chad looks around and sees many, but not all, students nodding with understanding.

Day Two: Chad realizes that the days of high school foreign language are long gone, and his instructor is moving at a good clip. Many of the students in this class have already had one or two years of high school French. Chad thinks to himself, *"This is going to be hard."* He slips further behind with each class.

Week Four: Chad is getting a **D** in French, passing by the skin of his teeth. Finally, the professor writes *"please see me"* on Chad's quiz. (It is an unusual request. Typically, professors don't ask to see students. Students are supposed to do the asking.) Chad talks to his professor, who recommends that Chad get a tutor. Chad takes the advice because he doesn't know what else to do.

Two days later: Chad meets with a French major, a senior, whom he likes a lot. He sees the tutor regularly. Chad's lucky. The university's language department provides tutoring as a free service. At another university, Chad might have to pay the tutor an hourly rate.

Week Seven: No question about it, the tutor has helped. Chad's quiz grades have improved, and Chad earns a **C** on the midterm test.

For the rest of the semester, he meets faithfully with his tutor. By the end of the semester, he has earned himself a solid **C** in the course. At first, Chad is greatly relieved. But then he realizes he has three more semesters of college French to go! He has to continue building on his weak background in French 001. *Is this the way it's going to be for three more semesters? Yes. Will the amount of time Chad spends with his tutor increase as courses get more difficult? Probably.*

Chad's alternative is to chalk up French 001 as a learning experience and sign up for Spanish 001 second semester, which he does. But Chad paid a price that affected more than his French course. In struggling to save his French grade, he robbed time from his other courses, so all of his grades suffered. Chad's **C** in French was not the only **C** he got. In his first semester in college, his grade point average was already low.

Dean's commentary

In the early days of the semester, Chad did what he always did in difficult situations: *He hoped somehow things would turn out okay.* Chad had never worked much in high school for grades, so he never thought about having to study harder and put in more hours than usual to keep up with a subject he knew nothing about.

Chad should have talked to his instructor or his college adviser after the first two or three days of the course. Either probably would have sized up Chad as being pretty clueless and recommended that he transfer to Spanish 001, which he could still do in the early days of the semester with his adviser's approval. Spanish 001 is where his two years of high school Spanish would have placed him. Chad's high school Spanish would have given him an easier transition into a college-level foreign language before the course started to move beyond his knowledge.

But because Chad didn't talk to his instructor or his adviser in the first two weeks, he didn't know any of this.

Other students in the class who had no French background did very well. Chad just didn't know how: He needed to put in more effort. Sure, learning French at a college pace was going to be more difficult than learning college Spanish and building on his background of high school Spanish, but he could have succeeded by improving his study effort. The good news is that Chad's tutor helped Chad hobble along and pass the course. But the bad news is that Chad used the tutor as a crutch, never really getting the idea that he still was not shouldering the responsibility for his own learning. The tutor created the outside-of-class learning experience that Chad could have — *and should have* — created for himself by studying more and putting in more effort.

But Chad's problem is far from over: Chad is typical of so many students who must take courses in sequence: like chemistry, math, and foreign language. French 002, 003, and 004 follow French 001. When you get behind in one course, it affects not only this semester but the next semester, and the semester after that.

Getting behind is deadly. It forces students to change their majors, their degree programs, and their career plans. It creates stress and that awful feeling of "always playing catch-up." Not controlling courses costs you time: It can add extra semesters and therefore extra cost to earning a degree. And it all happens because some students never learned how to start a semester, assign enough study time to each course, and get off to a strong and immediate start.

So jump-start ALL your courses every semester. Start studying on DAY ONE. Organize your time and your study strategies, look frequently at your calendar, and always be ahead of the game. If you think you're having trouble, see your teacher or counselor right away. You can never win the game of catch-up without paying the price somehow. What did Chad do? He hoped for a miracle. That never works.

Meredith
The battle of biology, retreat or advance?

As a first-semester college freshman, Meredith chose biology as the first of two science courses she was required to take for her degree. Not only was biology her favorite science in high school, she was also pretty sure that she wouldn't have to do much math in it, unlike what she'd heard about other science courses. (Meredith avoided math-related courses at all costs.)

In high school, Meredith liked dissecting animals and learning about the environment. She thought college biology would be more of the same. However, she discovered that in her college course, she was surrounded by biology majors, as well as students who planned to go on to medical and dental school. They were taking the course to learn, not about frogs and earthworms, but about the structure and function of cells. Meredith's first mistake was not carefully reading the course description in the college bulletin. Her second mistake? If she had looked at the course outline, she would have noticed that "frogs" weren't mentioned. Lastly, she was equally careless about looking through the textbook she bought for the course. She didn't open it until she heard about the first test.

Because she felt confident about her high school biology background, Meredith approached her college course the way she approached all of her courses — gradually. She only started thinking seriously about studying in the third week of the semester, after she had made friends with everyone on her dorm floor, signed up for lots of social clubs, and partied through the weekends. That's when she began to realize how different this material really was from her high school biology.

She hadn't read the course outline carefully in the first two weeks, and she was surprised to learn from another student that the first test was scheduled for Week Four. This was already Week Three. The instructor hadn't warned students about the upcoming test yet. He'd put the course schedule in writing, and he believed that students were supposed to keep track of such things.

Later, she told me about the test. She didn't know how to answer the first multiple-choice question, and by the time she reached question 50, she was sick to her stomach and asking herself, *"What do I do? Do I drop this course? I don't think that I can drop it. It's a requirement. I'm really messed up."* Her grade was a **D**.

Still, Meredith was determined, so she decided to try to turn her biology grade around. I told her that I thought she might recover, but this was her dilemma: She was going to have to make up for the studying she'd lost in the first three weeks of biology. At the same time, she was going to have to keep up with each day's new material for the class. It was going to mean lots of work.

There was another complication. The extra time Meredith spent on biology took study time away from her other four courses. She was going to have to risk low grades in her other courses to save biology. What's more, I was pretty sure Meredith was in much the same situation in her other courses: Behind! She had realized too late what she should have been doing during the first weeks of the semester. But she couldn't turn back the clock.

So Meredith dropped Biology and devoted that extra study time she gained without Biology to her other courses. The result was pretty good grades in her remaining courses. But she still had a **W** grade (showing she had **W**ithdrawn from Biology) on her record. That grade was a wake-up call for Meredith, and she was smart enough to hear it. Never again did she "take it easy" at the beginning of a semester.

Dean's commentary

Students want college courses to start out slowly like high school or middle school courses — and then *gradually* move more quickly and get harder. College courses are not like that. They start out fast and move at the same quick pace all semester long. Yet many students never quite understand that accelerated pace, so when the first major college test or assignment comes due, these students are not prepared. They are "behind" in the course. As a result, the grades on that first test or assignment tend to be low.

So, four weeks into the semester, students are already behind in learning the course material, and they've got a low grade. Now their problem is how to catch up, and the truth is that *in college courses, there is no catching up.* Students can't do anything to eliminate that first low grade. It's always going to act like an anchor and pull down their future grades. The chances of earning really excellent grades later in these courses are slim. Here's why: Students have missed learning the material in the early part of the course, and because of the quick pace of the course, they have little time to go back and learn what they've missed. They have to keep looking ahead, studying for each new day. Repairing the damage earlier in the course and keeping pace with new material is too much to do. Often, the result is dropping the course, which puts students behind in their whole degree program, making them add semesters to complete their college degree.

Studying a course is like constructing a building. You build it one story at a time. You begin with the foundation. Constructing a strong foundation creates a building that will last many years. However, if the foundation isn't strong, then the first story doesn't sit on a solid base. It teeters. None of the other stories will sit atop each other any better. So it is with learning: When you miss mastering the lessons early in a course, you've weakened the foundation for the rest of the course. The building is likely to crumble and fall.

Each building, each course, is under construction every semester. However, if you don't pay attention to constructing them well, they begin to topple over. As you divide your time, trying to save each building, with a little more cement here and a little more support there, you are always running from one teetering building to another, trying to prop them up. If, next semester, you must continue constructing one or two of these buildings — like moving to the next course in foreign language or math, your buildings sway even more. They are taller buildings trying to stand on a wobbly foundation. Eventually they will fall, and as they collapse, they may bring down the other buildings (courses) that stand around them.

Don't get behind in your courses. Poor foundations and low grades in first tests and assignments are a major reason that 25% of college freshmen don't return sophomore year. In fact, it's a mistake that becomes a pattern for lots of sophomores, juniors, and seniors. They repeat this mistake each semester. Because of their low grades, they are forced to drop courses, go to summer school or add extra semesters to make up classes, change their original college plans, and even lose their career dreams. Most can't figure out why it's happening. They just know that things have gotten "too hard."

High school is the time for you to develop those study behaviors and learning skills that college demands. They don't come automatically. They require time and effort. So keep in mind that as a college smart student, your "job of learning" is no different than the work that a serious athlete brings to a sport or the effort that a musician spends working with an instrument. To win the game or make great music takes time. And that time begins on the first day of each semester.

RU READY?

Practice talking with anyone who will listen.

Strategy 4
Knowing how to talk —
it's more than running up the phone bill

The best students know how to talk. They are good conversationalists. Good questioners and explainers. They are at ease talking, and they express themselves clearly — in class or out. They do more than simply repeat the latest clichés: "It was, I mean, like, so totally cool, you know." Students who talk well are usually noticed, liked, and remembered. Why? Because what they say is usually interesting or right or adds to the quality of the conversation. Good talkers never fall into the category of just another person. Frequently, they are leaders: They captain sports teams, hold offices in student government, and speak up in class. These students understand that by talking, they can make things happen. Most successful adults are good talkers. Talking well is a big deal.

Learn about yourself

Check each one that applies to you.

____ I am comfortable talking to my friends.

____ I can talk seriously with my parents.

____ I can comfortably talk to my friends' parents, even when my friends aren't around.

____ I can talk to teachers and others in authority with no problem.

____ I can talk to adults in general — in stores, the library, other public places — and not be self-conscious or stumble through my words.

____ I get easily flustered when I have to speak to people other than my close friends.

____ If I have a choice to talk or not, I prefer not to talk.

These days, there are a lot of *A* students around — more than ever before. Nearly 30%[†] of college-bound students graduate from high school with an *A+* or *A* average. There are huge numbers of *A-* students, too. So with more *A* students out there than ever, what makes some *A* students stand out from the others? There's maturity, self-confidence, and other qualities of character and personality. But one quality really separates the few from the many, and that's knowing how to communicate — to clearly express their thoughts to other people with ease and with purpose.

Be college smart. If you can speak to adults without peppering your speech with *ums, you knows,* and *likes* … if you can say *yes* rather than *yeah* to adults … *if you can look adults in the eye when you talk,* you will distinguish yourself from a large portion of the *A*-student population. Who will care? College-admissions counselors, financial-aid officers, faculty and administrators in college, academic advisors, and, later, potential employers.

[†] From *The American Freshman: National Norms for Fall 2005, American Council on Education, UCLA*

Talking is fundamental.

Talking is the primary way we exchange ideas, information, and feelings. If you stop to think about it, your days are filled with spoken words. If you added up the number of words that a typical person reads, writes, and speaks in a lifetime, spoken words would vastly outnumber words that are written or read.

Talking and real life. Talking makes things happen. When you talk, you explain things, you answer questions, you get people interested or excited about your ideas. You get yourself recognized. Ask any adult *who gets the highest raise or the promotion.* Usually, it's the people who know how to talk. Non talkers or poor talkers might hold jobs, but they often don't go anywhere in the work world. Generally, talkers are the people who know how to best communicate to the outside world what their business does. In one way or another, every job involves explaining something to others, clearly reporting results or giving directions. Talkers earn reputations as valuable contributors. Talkers are leaders. In many instances, skilled talkers are considered indispensable.

Face it. You can have all the knowledge and great ideas in the world, *but if you can't get your thoughts out into the world* — expressing them by talking with clarity and persuasion — *they will remain hidden.* That's why talking is so important. It determines, to a certain extent, who you are and who you will be.

What's talking? *"Talking,"* as I use the word here, does not simply mean saying words, like *"Pass the ketchup, please."* We all do that. We have to, just to get through our day-to-day lives. Talking, in the most complete sense of the word, means drawing on a reasonably developed vocabulary to communicate thoughts that are often complicated or complex. Talking well requires thinking and organization.

Talking also involves careful listening. How can you respond to people intelligently unless you understand what they are saying? Therefore, talkers typically listen very carefully to others. You rarely hear these students say, *"I don't remember the teacher saying that"* or *"I didn't know that was going to be on the test."*

Talking in the classroom. The next time you're in a classroom, take a good look at what's happening there. A teacher is talking to students about a subject. In fact, the teacher does most of the talking. But when students are asked questions, which students do most of the talking? Usually, it's the "best" students who are responding to or asking questions. Why? Talking helps these students understand their own thoughts. In other words, talking keeps their minds working. Remember the difference between students who think of their minds as containers and those who think of their minds as processors? Good talkers are always good processors.

Since talkers are involved in their courses, the material becomes more interesting to them. And because talkers usually have something intelligent or thought-provoking to say, they make the discussion more interesting for others, too. Talking relies on give and take: exchanging ideas. In a classroom with a lot of discussion, students are learning as much from each other as they do from the teacher. Talking is at the heart of learning.

Classes are social experiences where people feel invigorated because they're working with each other toward a particular goal — learning the subject. It's why students say, *"That class is really good."* Students leave these kinds of classes feeling that learning is exciting because everybody comes prepared so they can talk with focus, knowledge, and curiosity. Ask students which courses are boring, and they will describe courses in which intelligent talking is at a minimum.

This is important: Your education is not just about getting the right answers on test questions. Your education should include developing communication skills. One way to develop those skills is to *talk in the classroom: answer the teacher's questions, ask your own, and join in the discussion.* You should talk in all of your classes, not just those classes that deal specifically with speaking and communication skills. As you'll learn later in Strategy 5, talking in the classroom directly prepares you for the workplace.

What talking does for your mind. Talking sharpens your mind because you are constantly asking your brain to put your thoughts into words. And to do that, you have to choose good words and string them together in a way that makes it easy for any listener to understand. Besides making you an attentive listener, good talking also helps you become a better writer, because good writing is "talking" on the page, but with more formality.

Learning to talk is an altogether different process than writing. You think on your feet, and that means you have to gather your thoughts before you open your mouth. You do a split-second check that your thoughts are organized, and then you begin using words to express yourself. Sometimes you don't know what you're going to say until you hear yourself saying it. While teachers will work with you to improve your writing, you are going to have to work independently to become a good talker. Take the suggestions in this Strategy and practice!

Talkers to avoid. Some students talk all the time in class — they talk to each other, but not about the subject. Their behavior is rude to the teacher and distracts the students who sit around them. These students don't care about learning, at least for the moment. But when they don't do well in the class, they blame their low grades on the teacher or say the class "is boring." Complaining is their favorite kind of talking.

"Talkie" students love to recruit others to join their group and fool around. You need to keep a safe distance. Don't even sit near them. They'll make it hard for you to concentrate.

About writing

When you speak, you are thinking of *what* you are saying *as* you are saying it. Talking is a remarkable mental skill because it happens so quickly.

Writing is different. You put your thoughts down on paper, and then you have the time to sit back and evaluate what you have said. You have the time to choose the right word, revise a sentence to make it better, or organize the order of your sentences within a paragraph. Readers expect you to take that care and make that effort. And that means more than running a document through a spell-checker or grammar-checker.

A professional writer will tell you that quality writing is *rewriting*. The point is that each time you revise the paper, you are refining it. Some people call writing "wordsmithing." In the old days, blacksmiths would heat and hammer metals into shapes on an anvil, repeatedly dipping the metal into flames and pounding it until it took the right shape. That's what good writers do: They work the words until they take on the right shape. Doing so might take some sweat and mental muscle. Software can't do this kind of work.

Practice talking.

Language skills really involve writing, reading, talking, and listening. The best communicators are skilled in all four areas. To sharpen your talking and listening skills, try to do more of each. Here are a few ways to get in some practice time.

Talk with people of different ages. Any student can talk with friends about day-to-day stuff, but that talking is filled with a lot of repetition, a lot of the latest and most popular phrases, and probably as much body language as real language. That's fine when you're talking to your friends. However, skilled talkers communicate well not only with their friends, but also with —

- Teachers
- Employers
- Parents
- Friends' parents

- Grandparents
- Neighbors
- Store clerks
- Younger children

- Physicians
- Dentists
- Coaches
- Senior citizens

Talk with your friends about semi-serious topics. You talk to these people all the time. Every now and then, spend some time talking about topics other than who's breaking up with whom. These kinds of topics will expand your skills:

- Why you liked a certain movie or book
- Why your sports team won a particular game
- Your personal interests/activities, like computers, music, cars, or fashions
- A story in the national news
- A local political issue or sporting event
- Something you're learning in a course
- Your plans, hopes, and dreams
- What colleges you are thinking about attending

Talk to the people around you. Talk to your adult neighbors — and, yes, your parents and their friends. If your mother's best friend is an accountant, a career that interests you, you've got a perfect topic of conversation. Try to talk to her *intelligently* about what she does. Begin by asking a question. As you listen to her, see if her description fits what you think an accountant does. Ask about the personal traits needed to be an accountant as well as the math skills. Does she like it? What are the best things about the job? The worst? What advice would she give you based on her experience? The conversation will sharpen your talking and listening skills. You'll also learn a thing or two that might encourage or discourage you about this career path.

Talk to yourself. Consider this: *Thinking* is talking to yourself. You know that voice you hear inside your head? You're *talking* to yourself. It's a soundless talk you use so you can hear what you are thinking and get your thoughts straight. Why is it that better talkers are also frequently better thinkers? For the simple reason that their internal voices organize and sharpen their thoughts. That's why you stop to think before you answer a question in class. Listen to your internal voice. Does it express your thoughts logically? Can you state them clearly, choose the right words, and get to the point? All this takes practice. Start thinking in full thoughts and sentences.

> **Be college smart.** Talking well builds your mind just like working out builds muscle on an athlete. Even if you have a long way to go to become a good talker, practice is the only way to help you steadily improve.

Expand your vocabulary.

Life is filled with complexities and shades of meaning. To understand it all requires knowledge and intelligence. That's why you're in school.

To use the knowledge you have learned, you have to be able to communicate it to others, which means being skilled in writing and talking. A good vocabulary is basic to both. Work on developing your vocabulary! Don't get stuck in a life that is limited because you can express yourself only in very simple ways. Pay attention to unfamiliar words when you read them or hear them. Look them up and write them down in a specific place. Regularly look at this growing word list and try to use these words. You'll be surprised how many new words you have "collected."

Use a dictionary and thesaurus in your study place. Yes, it takes a little time to look up words, but it's a good way to broaden your vocabulary.

Small vocabularies can choke off opportunities in your life. Being in command of a large vocabulary helps you achieve in a complicated and competitive world.

Talking right now

Yes, talking is important to your future and your career, but it's also vital to you right now in school. This Strategy on **Talking** and the two Strategies that follow, **Talking to Teachers and Talking to Your Guidance Counselor**, are extremely important, but often neglected. The next two Strategies will explain why.

Talking your way into your future

What do you want for yourself? To have a passive, quiet life that makes you a spectator? Or to have a dynamic, stimulating life in which you lead and influence people? Talking is the primary way you express who you are, what you think, and how you think. Talking is the greatest expression of *you* — your personality, your character, and your intelligence. Being a good talker always gives you an advantage.

Listen to Dr. Bob —

Why you need to practice this Strategy for college

Talking in the college classroom is just as essential to learning as taking part in discussions in the high school classroom.

- Can you participate in class and talk with the intelligence expected in a college classroom?

- Are your listening skills sharp enough to understand your professor's presentations, called lectures? Often, this information is not contained in your textbook.

- Can you follow and join in the class discussions so that you say something insightful? (You've heard students who try to talk in class but whose comments only prove that they've missed the point of the discussion.)

- Do you talk well enough to give a college-level presentation in front of the class?

- When your college course outline states that 20% of your grade depends on class participation, will you be able to handle that?

Talking becomes important in day-to-day ways in college, too. Remember: You are the one who takes care of you. Talking well and easily will help you get things done.

- Not on the class list for Chemistry? You have to go to the Registrar's Office and clear up the problem. Can you do that?

- Want to change your major (area of study) or your degree program? Schedule an appointment with your adviser to discuss this important matter.

- You're having a health problem. (Mom's not around.) You need to make an appointment at the campus health center. Can you describe the problem clearly and in detail?

- Your meal card won't scan. Find out who to see about it. Go straighten it out.

- Your roommate is driving you crazy! This is a major personal problem. Better sit down and talk it out with your roommate or your Resident Adviser.

- Having trouble with math? You can't just go into your instructor's office and say, "I don't get it." To get help, you have to be more specific.

In all of these instances — and a hundred more I can think of — you have to be able verbally to handle yourself. Find the words. Be clear. Be organized in your presentation. Be persuasive if you have to plead your case. You can't do that if you can't look people in the eyes and make yourself understood

Words, words, words. At a very basic level, that's what your education and learning is about. So never leave words behind you in your school locker. Besides taking part in intelligent conversations with other intelligent people, make sure you read books like novels or books about your favorite sports or hobbies. Read newspapers and magazines. Words! You need them. Where would you be without them!

PSST! Don't forget to read the highlighted sections. Process them and then practice your talking by telling someone about them! You're also almost halfway through the Strategies. Keep going. You're building skills that will shape your future.

Up close and personal
Sara and college interviews

Sara was used to being right. Sarah was super intelligent, a high school senior. She had a 4.0 grade point average and a *perfect* composite score of 36 on her ACT. She could have done the work at any college in the country. Many would have probably offered her significant scholarships. But when it came to talking, Sara couldn't carry on a conversation with adults. She would stammer and mumble and look at her feet.

In her junior year, she applied to the best colleges in the nation. All the schools set up interviews with her in the fall of her senior year. Top colleges want to talk with students who apply for admission. These colleges also want to see teacher recommendations. Prestigious institutions can afford to be picky about the students they take — especially now and in the next several years because there are so many college-bound students to choose from.

During these interviews, admissions representatives want to converse with applicants to measure their personal qualities. These schools want interesting young people as well as those with good grades: students who are poised conversationalists. Sara could not hold up her end of the conversation. So despite her genius, her grades, and her scores, she never made it past the interview stage of any of her applications to top schools.

Some of the interviewers may already have been suspicious of Sara because her letters of recommendation were not what they should have been. Her teachers did not praise Sara for her in-class performance or class leadership. They could not say that she sparked classroom discussions or contributed to the quality of the class. *While she was intellectually remarkable, her accomplishments were all private, like writing papers and scoring well on tests.*

Sara went to a college that was good, but not exceptional. In doing so, she missed out on the opportunity to exchange ideas with a student body of her intellectual equals. A degree from one of the well-known institutions could have opened dozens of opportunities for her in life.

Dean's commentary

Of all the Strategies in this book that define a college smart student, this one is the most often overlooked. Why? Because all students think that they can talk. They do it all the time with their friends.

I use Sara's story here because in spite of her great promise, her inability to talk hurt her. Not being able to talk hurts *all* students. But the damage is not confined to school.

Talking is a life skill that is valued in the work world. Sara's inability to speak well will continue to follow her when she interviews for jobs and seeks promotions. Learn from Sara. People don't suddenly, magically, or effortlessly learn to speak well. Talking, like any other skill, requires practice. Begin developing this skill now. **RU READY?**

I can get help by asking.

Talking to teachers —
why enter "forbidden territory"

If school were a sport, your teacher would be your coach. In fact, your teacher IS your coach in this intellectual athletic event called school. He or she explains the details of the game (the subject) and can help you build the talents you need to play (study skills). Your academic coach also evaluates you during practices (how well you are doing in class) and analyzes your game performance (your tests). Academic coaches (teachers) are specialists who know many ways to help you achieve your personal best. How do you get the most out of your teachers? Read on.

Learn about yourself

Check all that apply to you.

I talk to teachers—

_____ never. Not under any circumstances.

_____ when I'm in some sort of grade trouble.

_____ whenever I think I can argue for more points on a test.

_____ when a teacher starts a conversation with me.

_____ when I don't understand a concept presented in class or in the textbook.

_____ when I need help preparing for a test.

_____ whenever the opportunity arises.

Check the answer(s) that best describe(s) your attitude:

I view talking to teachers as —

_____ really "not cool."

_____ a sign of trying to manipulate the teacher to get a better grade.

_____ something that might leave me open to criticism from friends.

_____ a neutral action — it's not a big deal.

_____ a natural part of my school day.

_____ a way to help me learn more and better.

_____ a terrifying experience.

Teacher as academic coach

This Strategy started out by comparing a teacher to an athletic coach. It's a valid comparison in a couple of ways: You're not the only one on the team (your class), and your coach directs all the players on the team. But just as coaching will advance you in a sport, if you make the effort to build a good relationship with your teacher, you can really accelerate your academic progress and enrich your learning experience. That's because your teacher's comments are aimed at you *individually*. It's talk that is focused on you, your needs, and your interests.

Adding to the classroom experience

When you leave a movie with your friends, what happens? Most likely, you talk about the movie all the way home. You chatter about the parts you liked best or any details that captured your imagination. You compare the movie with other movies like it. You talk about the actors. Have you ever walked out of a movie and not said a word about it? Probably not. Even if you didn't like the movie, you talked about why.

It's the same with class. *If you've been involved in the class discussion,* your mind doesn't just shut off because the bell rings and class is over. Do you have unanswered questions? Does some point not make sense? Do you wonder about something you just learned? Do you disagree with something the teacher said?

Go talk to the teacher as you would talk to your movie-going friends. Talk about what's on your mind. You might ask for a further explanation to clear up a point. Or you may suddenly discover that something said in this class ties in to another class. For example, are you reading a novel in your English class that takes place in the same country and time period you are studying in history? Can you see how the two courses relate to each other? Talk to your teachers about how one class sheds light on the other. Your education is always more interesting when you notice relationships between and among your courses.

The value of one-on-one relationships

When you, as a student, talk to teachers about the course material or share insights about connections you see among courses, the things you've learned become more real, more interesting, and more memorable. You are exploring ideas out loud. It's like talking with your friends about the movie you've just seen. When courses become more interesting to you, you'll do better in them. You'll read chapters more carefully and take your assignments more seriously. Talking is the key to an exciting learning experience. Silence makes learning impossible — and boring.

Talking with purpose

You could go through a course and never have a private conversation with a teacher, but here are some opportunities you'd be missing:

- *Filling the knowledge gaps.* Every student has them. Talk about those not-so-clear things you only "sort of" know *before* they appear on a test or prevent you from understanding whatever material builds on them.

- *Satisfying your need to know more.* Are you already a regular talker in class? Talking to teachers outside of class fills your need to know more, and you don't have to worry about dominating class discussions.

- *Getting answers to questions you don't have time to ask in class.* Think about those questions you'd like to ask in class, but you don't ask them, because the class has to keep moving. Write your questions down, and then go see the teacher outside of class.

- *Reviewing your tests and getting individualized pointers.* If the teacher has gone over the test in class, you already know WHAT questions you got wrong. After class, the teacher can tell you privately WHY you got them wrong. What's more, the teacher can give you pointers about how to avoid repeating these mistakes in the future. As you have more and more conversations with teachers about tests, you'll become a better test taker. (More about this is in Strategy 9.)

- *Learning how to prepare for next tests.* Let's say that you didn't do very well in the last test, and you go to your teacher to find out why. The teacher points to a section of the test where you lost several points. You say that you've never seen that material before. It wasn't in your notes. The teacher replies that the information was in the textbook. You didn't read the chapter because the teacher said she wouldn't have time to discuss it in class. Now you know that the teacher considers anything fair game for tests: old assignments, notes, video presentations, textbooks, handouts, and guest speakers. You've just gotten wiser about how to get ready for the next test.

Walls that separate

Now you understand all the reasons that you should develop a relationship with your teachers. *Will you?* While most student athletes develop good working relationships with their coaches, many students shy away from developing the same kind of relationships with their teachers. Why? They don't feel comfortable talking to teachers. Over the years, a wall has been built between teacher and student. Here's how it happens.

When you were in grade school, you most likely spent your entire day in a single room with a single teacher. You knew this teacher very well, and the teacher knew you well, too. Now that you are older and moving from teacher to teacher to learn different subjects, you no longer have that same kind of close relationship with each. Because you know your teachers less well, you've become less comfortable around them and cannot talk as easily with them. Other obstacles also come into play to prevent building a good relationship with your teachers.

Obstacle #1. It's up to you to make the first move. At the same time that you've lost your former comfortable feeling with teachers, you not only have to talk to them, you have to *approach* them. It's up to you to make the first move. Why? Your teacher may have many, many students, but not all of them want to develop a one-on-one relationship with the teacher, so you must take the initiative to let the teacher know that you do. The first time you approach a teacher, you might have to use some courage.

Why don't all students want a one-on-one relationship? Obstacles #2 and #3 sometimes get in the way.

Obstacle #2. Cool conduct. Some students have a list of unwritten rules about "cool conduct," and they believe that talking with teachers is unacceptable behavior. These students can pressure you to accept and go along with their opinions. Some students have a hard time resisting that kind of pressure, and so they resist talking to teachers. It's the students' loss.

Obstacle #3. Not at ease talking. Then there's your comfort level in talking with adults. You read about that in the last Strategy. How at ease do you feel talking with teachers? Can you find words and put them into sentences? Or do you stammer and stumble? Which brings up a good question...

When did talking become so difficult?

When very young children begin to talk, the family celebrates. If these children grow up in a family with many word-based interests like reading, going to movies and plays, and spending time in dinner discussions, children's language develops at an amazing rate.

However, somewhere along the way to high school, many students stop developing their ability to talk. They don't continue to learn more words. They don't try to speak in more mature kinds of sentences. Their language and speaking skills come to a grinding halt.

When the part of the brain that handles language is not continually used or excited by new challenges, it becomes lazy. Much of it falls asleep. The result? Your young mind that once handled language with ease now has verbal arthritis and decides to just sit around in a nonverbal chair, doing nothing.

Get the verbal part of your brain out of that easy chair and get it bending its knees! You're going to need it. Your academic success depends on your ability to communicate. Just think about it for a minute. Everything you do to learn is connected to words in one form or another: reading and writing, talking and listening. (Math is just another language you need to learn.)

Students get the wrong idea about the need to talk, because *so far,* they have been graded much more on their reading, writing, and listening skills. True, "class discussion" is a basic method of teaching. However, nearly all of your tests ask you to write rather than speak. That's why so many students with consistently high grades have less than adequate talking skills. And that's why so many students dread giving an oral report or a presentation.

How about you? Can you speak easily and well to people one on one or in groups? If not, you need to wake up that verbal part of your brain and exercise it before it's too late. College and your success in the workplace depend on your ability to express yourself clearly. More about this in a couple of pages. For now, we have to return to the high school problem of dealing with the wall between students and teachers.

Getting to the other side of the wall

Any or all of the three obstacles mentioned earlier become a wall that keeps today's students very separate from teachers. This wall has existed in the minds of some students for a long time.

How do you get to that other side of the wall? Get a ladder? How about simply walking through the door that's right in front of you? The door is the teacher's willingness to talk to students.

Most teachers, even the ones you consider unfriendly, want to make it easy for you to talk to them if you will take the first step.

Contrary to what you or your friends may think, most teachers like to talk to students, in or out of class. Teachers are in the education business because they like discussing a certain subject with interested young people. It's very rare to find a teacher who doesn't like talking with students.

Even the teachers who seem formal in the classroom can often quickly drop the formality as the end-of-class bell rings. Many students have found that these "unapproachable" teachers are very willing to talk face to face. In fact, some seem to enjoy private conversations more than talking to an entire class.

Be college smart. Teachers, like students, come in all sizes, shapes, and personalities. And just like everyone else, talking face to face comes easier to some teachers than others. However, even teachers who are less comfortable talking outside of class will make time for you. Just keep in mind that some days are busier than others for teachers. Don't take it personally if a teacher can't speak to you on the spur of the moment. Just schedule another time.

Talking as processing information

There's talking with the teacher outside of class, and there's talking to the teacher in class. This second kind of talking can take the form of asking or answering questions — or participating in class discussions. If you're not taking an active part in class discussions, you may as well watch the class on a monitor.

What happens when you enter a class discussion? You're no longer just a spectator. A good discussion is a little like playing in a soccer game. However, instead of a ball, ideas are kicked back and forth. You express your opinion, challenge someone else's, argue the evidence, build a case to support your view, bounce ideas off each other, solve problems, and reach conclusions.

You'll find that when you're involved in class discussions, learning becomes lively and interesting. It's the difference between watching a soccer game and being a key player. Your mind is active and productive — and the time flies. You won't find yourself watching the clock.

Remember the layers of learning? Talking in class is one of them.

An urgent need to talk

Don't let talking remain an undeveloped part of your learning. Talking is a LIFE SKILL. Everything you feel and think, want or need, understand or question in life depends on your ability to talk. Talking in class and talking with teachers are mental exercises that will prepare you for building personal relationships as well as succeeding in college, getting a job, and advancing a career.

In college. Many professors grade students on class participation. And when a course depends on only two tests and a paper, *how well you talk in class* contributes greatly to your final grade.

In the workplace. Most jobs depend on committees, departments, or teams working together to solve problems or come up with new ideas. Having a keen mind is valued. So is being able to talk clearly and directly about your ideas. Can you grab onto a project or problem, analyze it, and then debate the merits of different approaches or solutions? Those who actively involve themselves in a daily learning process and who can express themselves are going places. The rest of the employees will sit and take notes — sort of what the nontalkers do in class right now.

To recap

Talking to teachers in and outside of class helps you come at learning from several different directions. The more directions, the better.

Talk in class. Don't just sit there. Ask questions and contribute to class discussion. You have plenty of opportunities to speak in class — if you take the chance!

Talk with your teacher after class just as you would talk to an adult about a movie you just saw.

Make an appointment to talk in private. Schedule a face-to-face conversation early on in the course. Once you've had the first conversation, make it a habit. You'll find that the course will get more interesting to you as you get to know the teacher.

Talk when you need help. If you are struggling in a course, get help. And do it right away. Don't wait! Your teacher will give you helpful advice to manage a subject, get through rough spots, or tell you about group help sessions. But you have to take the first step.

Don't forget email and voicemail. If you're having a hard time connecting with a teacher, try email, or leave a voicemail. It may not be as personal as talking, but if you need a quick answer, either may do the trick.

Stay connected.

The more lines of communication you build between you and your teachers, the more personally involved you'll be — and the more enjoyable all your courses will be. And when things are interesting and enjoyable, you have a greater chance of getting the highest possible grades along with the broadest possible knowledge.

The ideal teaching-learning situation is one teacher for each student. That may have occurred within the privileged classes a century or so ago, but not anymore.

Today, you have to create your own learning situation and make it as rich as possible. Whether your class has 5 or 55 students, developing multiple lines of communication takes intelligence, maturity, and effort. But your good efforts will give you greater control of your education and be followed by the highest grades you can get. And those high grades will get you to places you want to go. Just remember, *keep talking*.

Do you recall Chad's problems with French in **The first two weeks?** All of his frustration and worry, his low grades, and his need for a tutor could have been avoided. All he needed to do was talk to his professor in the first two or three days of the course and explain how lost and confused he felt. The professor would have set him straight on how much time he had to invest in the class. If he was unwilling, the professor would have recommended that Chad see his adviser and change courses. Instead, Chad wasted his time, the course, and his parents' money. One important conversation could have spared him all of this grief.

Listen to Dr. Bob —

Why you need to practice this Strategy for college

Remember what we have already said: At college, you are the person who takes care of yourself. College professors post their office hours (times when students can come in to talk about assignments or get help). When you get a paper or test with a grade lower than what you wanted, or you're having trouble, *you must take the initiative* to see your professor during office hours. Rarely will a professor approach you about your progress or your grades.

- Not sure if your thesis statement will meet the requirement for your next English paper? Visit your professor and show him your statement. Get his approval. Don't risk a low grade because you didn't follow directions.

- Does a particular course really interest you? Go talk to your professor during office hours to learn more about this area of study. Find out what other courses are offered in this area. Which ones could you take?

- Disappointed in your last test grade in chemistry? See your professor during office hours. You can ask her to go over those troublesome formulas step by step so you understand them.

- Thinking of applying for an internship related to your area of study? Most require interviews. Will you be able to persuade the interviewer that you are better than the other students competing for the internship? Talk to your academic adviser.

Some classes can be so large that professors don't even know your name, much less worry about you or your grades. It is your responsibility to go to them for help. In fact, they are just waiting for interested students to come and talk to them. But you must make the first move. *Now's the time to get used to talking to teachers.* They can be a great help to students. Jeff's story illustrates how one thing leads to another when you begin to talk.

PSST! Go back and reread the highlighted passages. As you finish reading each Strategy, think about ways you can put its ideas to work right now, while these pages are fresh in your mind. Take action, and take action right away! Choose a teacher, and go talk about one of the topics in this Strategy.

Up close and personal

Jeff starts to talk and finds a career.

A student's life can change very quickly. That's what happened with Jeff, who was a very good but rather quiet student. His high school teachers liked him, and Jeff was serious about college. When he graduated from high school and it came time to choose a program of courses to study in college, he didn't know where to begin. His parents wanted him to pursue a very practical college major, like business administration. They thought a degree in business would give their son lots of jobs to choose from after he graduated from college. Since Jeff had never had any conversations with teachers or counselors about what to study in college, he let his parents be his guide.

Having been accepted by a business program of a nearby university, Jeff went off to college. He adjusted rather easily. He was soon taking accounting, finance, and marketing courses. For his degree, he also needed to take a social science course. He chose psychology because, even though he had never told anyone, he had always been interested in psychology: why people do what they do, and why they feel the way they feel.

From the first day of his psychology course, Jeff's life began to change. He was enthusiastic about everything he heard in class and everything he read. He couldn't get enough of it. He was the first to volunteer comments in class and the first to answer the questions of his professor. He had never been so active in a class before. He even began to see the relationship between psychology and business. Business is about selling and buying. If businesses understood the psychology of consumers — why people buy — these businesses could better figure out what products people wanted and how to sell these items.

His enthusiasm for his psychology course was apparent in everything he did as a student. Being excited about one course made him more interested in his other courses. It was like having a wonderfully contagious disease that infected everything he touched. Intellectually, he had never felt more alive. He quickly went from a rather quiet person to a student who was expressive and conversational.

But the best was yet to come. He decided to major in psychology and minor in business, which meant his main area of study would be psychology and his second area of study would be business. In order to do that, he had to transfer from one academic area to another. At a university, it's called changing colleges. That's when I first met Jeff. I had to give him permission to enter our college.

He told me about his new academic interest, and his extraordinary excitement was apparent. I told him to talk with his psychology professor about officially changing his program of study. He saw me again in a few weeks. When he had spoken with her, the professor had told Jeff how much she appreciated his contributions to class discussions. She encouraged him to continue taking psychology courses and even invited him to come back and talk with her as his courses and plans developed.

In a very short period of time, Jeff and his professor became good friends. She eventually helped him choose a particular area of psychology for graduate study as well as several universities to apply to. She wrote one of his letters of recommendation for graduate school.

I saw Jeff at graduation, and he told me where he was going to do his graduate study, and how happy he was that his academic life had become so exciting. I told him that it was all because he had followed his personal interests and started to "talk" about them. That's where students always find success, enjoyment, and satisfaction.

Dean's commentary

Was it Jeff's excitement about psychology that made him an eager conversationalist? Or was it his newfound confidence in his ability to talk that made him feel so great about psychology? No matter. It all came together, and it was his professor's personal interest in him that made it all work.

Talking counts, and the sooner you start doing it, the better off you'll be, as a student and as a person. So the next time you sit quietly in the back of a classroom, wondering what you're doing there, think of Jeff. Move to the front of the room tomorrow, start asking and answering questions, and go talk to your teacher. Like Jeff, you may discover your life. **RU READY?**

Talking with your guidance counselor —
everyone needs regular guidance and advice, even you

Are you taking the right college-prep courses? Are you sure you're taking the right approach to studying — or preparing for the SAT or ACT? What about selecting colleges that might be best for you? Or do you need some help with the complex college-application process? Your guidance counselor is another specialist or coach who can direct you through these and all kinds of academic situations.

Lost your focus? It can happen to anyone. Why are you in school anyway? Are personal matters complicating your life as a student? Do you have problems that are hard to explain? Your guidance counselor can help. Don't be foolish and think that you can take care of everything yourself. Everyone, especially students, needs advice and guidance — not just occasionally, but regularly.

Learn about yourself

Check all that apply to you.

How do you relate to your guidance counselor?

____ I think guidance counselors are mainly for students in trouble or who have learning problems.

____ I see my counselor once or twice each semester to discuss everything from grades to study habits, to college plans.

____ When I see my counselor, I don't know what to say.

____ My counselor doesn't really say much to me, so my appointments are short.

____ When I get ready for college applications and stuff like that, then I'll talk to my counselor more often.

____ I make sure to see my counselor when I need to have forms signed.

____ My counselor is always helpful, and the Counseling Office has good reference materials.

____ What's a guidance counselor?

Guidance? Who needs it?

Having been involved in counseling programs for many years, I could never understand why students were reluctant to talk to high school or college counselors. Counselors are the very people who can help students do everything — from getting higher grades and solving personal problems to planning for their futures.

I always assumed that some students were just too nervous to talk about their studies, and other students just didn't want to bother. For some, it was a combination of both. But there's another explanation. It's even more basic. And I didn't really understand it until my son ignored my advice to see his counselor about a couple of important school issues. I asked him why he kept putting it off. Finally, he told me he didn't want to be seen in the guidance office because his friends never talked to their counselors. According to my son, *the only students who go to the counseling office are the ones in trouble or who have learning problems.* He couldn't have been more mistaken.

Whether you know it or not, your guidance counselor is one of your best learning resources and academic friends. Yet many students consider going to counselors as something of a nuisance or a sign of weakness. They argue…

- *"Who has the time? What will I talk about?"* True, exchanging ideas does take time, but it's another way to practice your talking skills. As for topics of conversation, there are hundreds. You'll find some at the end of this Strategy.

- *"Who needs it? I do fine on my own. Needing advice is a sign of immaturity."* That's wrong. Take my word for it! Just the opposite is true, as the next section explains.

A counselor at work

Let me tell you about my son's friend, Katie. She was overscheduled. Her sophomore year in high school, she was on the swim team as well as working a part-time job. She wasn't getting enough sleep, and she got sick. What started as a bad cold turned into pneumonia. She missed lots of school and tests. She fell behind in her homework in all of her courses. She and her parents turned to the guidance counselor for help.

Once the counselor found out about her problems, he contacted all of Katie's teachers and explained her situation. He worked with Katie's teachers to plan out ways that she could get help with assignments at home, he rearranged due dates so she could catch up, and he helped Katie finish out the semester. He solved Katie's problems and reduced her stress.

Counselors can accomplish many things for you — including acting as your representative when you need one. Guidance counselors understand how the school works, so they can easily get things done that would be hard for you to do on your own.

But the value of a guidance counselor is not limited to helping out in emergencies such as Katie's. Generally speaking, people who make the best decisions make those decisions after getting advice from experts. Adults go to professionals, like stockbrokers or attorneys, for specialized advice. That's because intelligent adults value expert information. *So should you.*

To improve your life, get into the habit of consulting people in the know: experts and professionals. One of those people is your guidance counselor. Guidance counselors listen to you, understand what you are saying, *even when you don't,* and give you straightforward advice. Here's something else you should understand: You might think that your life is filled with problems, yet even when you fix just one part of your school life, *all* parts of your life get better. When that happens, you become more motivated to get your entire life together — something that's hard to do in the complicated world of being a student.

Your *personal* guide

True, part of a guidance counselor's job is getting "troubled" students back on track. Yet a counselor's larger job is helping *all* students stay on-track and advance themselves toward graduation. Counselors have a unique view of what's going on in your school. They have an overview of all course offerings, and they know about requirements. Because they have talked with so many students over a long time, they can offer you study tips or strategies for course scheduling — or help you when you're simply going through a hard time. And having a hard time does not only mean having difficulty with one or two courses. It can mean getting through those hard times when you feel burned-out or when you're frustrated because you don't know where you and your education are going.

To figure things out, counselors often have to ask questions about your personal as well as your academic life. The two are always interconnected. Many students don't want to answer personal questions. Some students have family or health problems that embarrass them. Some don't want to reveal that their education is not at the top of their "to-do" list. Others worry that counselors won't keep conversations confidential. They will. Counselors are bound to confidentiality by the rules of their profession and by law, just like doctors and lawyers. So be honest with your counselor. Talk about everything that affects your education and your plans for the future. It's the kind of two-way communication that solves problems.

Here's a warning: Counselors are human like the rest of us, so some may be incompetent and uncooperative — just like some students. If you have had a few conversations with your counselor and you've failed to get some communication going, ask to change counselors. Just remember this, though, before you change: A conversation is a two-way street. If you haven't gone into these appointments *prepared to talk honestly about specific topics,* no counselor will seem competent.

However, when your efforts are sincere and your topics of conversation are well-planned, but *still* your counselor seems confused or never seems to have time for you, then it's time to change counselors. See an assistant principal.

What you can talk to your counselor about: practically everything

In **The first two weeks**, I said you should spend some time reviewing and planning as the new semester gets underway. You should review last term and evaluate its ups and downs. Then look ahead to the new term to figure out how to turn the downs into ups — and keep the ups "up there." (Chin up, you'll figure it out!) A review-and-plan conversation is a good one to introduce (or reintroduce) yourself to your guidance counselor. Here are some other topics for talk:

_____ what courses you like and why

_____ what courses you don't like and why

_____ what courses are giving you trouble and how to overcome it

_____ trouble with a teacher — how to solve the problem

_____ how you are doing in fulfilling your graduation requirements

_____ whether you should take honors or Advanced Placement courses. Which ones? How many can you reasonably handle?

_____ what your course schedule should be next year

_____ selecting and applying to colleges

_____ areas you might want to study in college

_____ careers that interest you

You get the idea. Use the following blanks to make a list of any special concerns that you have right now. Then make an appointment with your guidance counselor. Right now. Forget about what your friends do. This is your education, and you're going to make the best of it with the best guidance you can get. List your special concerns here:

_____

_____

_____

_____

_____

Your high school's Guidance Center should be as familiar to you as your school's cafeteria. It's a place you want to visit regularly, not only to consult your counselor, but also to look at the wide variety of materials and announcements every college smart high school student should know about. Your Guidance Center will have information, whether in hard copy or on a computer, about SATs and ACTs, Advanced Placement courses, colleges, college applications, college scholarships, and financial aid. A Guidance Center is one of the best places to help you get ahead.

Your Guidance Center also sponsors various informative meetings and programs like College Nights, Career Fairs, and other programs that give you the opportunity to meet and talk to people about various occupations.

Want to go to an Open House at a nearby college? Maybe your Guidance Center will take a van full of students just like you. The college smart student goes to every program and is open-minded when listening to people talk about careers — even when friends say, *"Who would ever want a job as a _____?"* (You fill in the blank.) You never know. Small-animal dentistry may be just up your alley!

Listen to Dr. Bob —

Why you need to practice this Strategy for college

In college, you are assigned an adviser. This is the person who helps you plan and then approves your course schedule each semester so you graduate on time. However, advisers can do so much more. *Want to talk about a possible major (an area of study)?* This is the person to talk to. *Thinking about dropping a course?* You'd better get some advice first. From where? Your adviser, of course. If you drop the course, you might need your adviser's signature. *Want to graduate on time?* Your adviser will help you plan. *Have a personal problem and don't know who to see about it?* Start with your college adviser. There are resources on campus, and your adviser can refer you to them. *Need a tutor?* Your adviser knows where to find one. Working with any kind of adviser is a skill worth developing, one you can use throughout your life.

Students who have good working relationships with their college advisers face fewer complications and frustrations in completing their degrees and graduating on time. Start building a relationship with your high school guidance counselor now. It will prepare you to work with your college adviser.

PSST! Don't forget to go back and read the highlights! Choose a topic that's meaningful to you from pages 93-94. Then call to make an appointment with your guidance counselor.

Up close and personal

Elena doesn't understand her problem.

Elena did everything right to get ready for college. She took college-prep courses and worked hard to get the best grades. Early in her sophomore year, she started talking to her counselor and teachers about her college plans and interests. She selected six colleges she really liked, researched them on the Internet, and read about them in college reference books. She visited each college and talked with the right people to make sure she knew everything she could about the areas of study they offered, degree programs and requirements, dorm life, and financial aid.

She took time to prepare for the ACT and got great scores.

When her senior year started, Elena was ready to apply. She got strong letters of recommendation, and she was finally accepted by all six colleges, with very generous financial-aid packages. After some serious conversations with her counselor and parents, she made a good choice. She couldn't wait for the summer to end and for college to begin.

College began for Elena, but after one week, she knew something was wrong. Because she was used to talking with teachers and counselors, she talked first with her Dorm Adviser, who referred her to me.

In my first conversation with her, I couldn't believe anything could be wrong. Elena told me about her academic background and about her college plans. It was a pleasure to talk with such a completely friendly, well-spoken, and mature student.

When we got down to her problems, I told her to be simple and direct. Elena was. She said, *"I don't like it here."* I asked what, in particular, was wrong. Was it the dorm, her roommate, any of her courses? She said, *"No, it's great here. It's everything I thought it would be. But,"* she went on, *"I don't like being here. I don't know why. I'm uneasy all the time, I'm sad being away from my family, I feel like at any minute I will just suddenly leave and go home."*

Elena was homesick, very seriously homesick — to a degree I had not seen before. All college students experience some homesickness. For most students, the feeling lasts a few days or a couple weeks. However, once the loneliness and discomfort caused by being away from home are replaced by new friendships, new familiarities, and new comforts, the homesickness disappears.

I asked Elena to work with me, and I would help her get adjusted. I first phoned all of her professors and told them she needed a little encouragement. Then I invited Elena to come to my office each day and sit in my outer office to study. Part of her problem was that she needed a place "to belong." The office staff knew her, so the place was friendly and quiet, but no one bothered her. This temporary study place had helped other students feel rooted until they could move on to the library or a more traditional study place.

I encouraged her to make an appointment with the Counseling Center. And there were some other people I knew who were good at making students feel at home. I told her see them all, and she did.

After two weeks Elena saw me again and told me how grateful she was for all the help she received: *"People have been so supportive. I feel like they really care."* *"They do,"* I said. *"We very much want students like you at our school."* But I could see by the look in her eyes that her deepest feelings had not changed. So I asked, *"If I were to give you a ticket home right now would you take it?"* She said, *"Without a second thought."* I said, *"Okay, we did our best. Now it's time to do what you want, because this is your choice."*

The next day, Elena and her mother were in my office to finalize her complete withdrawal from the college. I told them I was going to refund their tuition because Elena was experiencing a health problem, and they shouldn't be charged for something they couldn't anticipate.

Elena left my office feeling very grateful for the help of many people, very relieved that she was going home, very eager to deal with her problem with a psychologist, and very determined to start planning for a new college experience.

Dean's commentary

Elena represents many college students who, for any number of reasons, are not ready to start college.

At first glance, you might look at Elena's situation and feel sorry for her. But a second glance should make you understand that, under the circumstances, things could not have worked out better for her. The next time you really feel like you're in an impossible situation, think of Elena and start talking with people in the know — experts. You'll be surprised how even awful situations can be managed and solved with the right advice and counsel.

About being homesick. Homesickness can be a terrible adjustment problem for some students. Everything is new: roommates, cafeteria food, sleep patterns, and a class schedule unlike any the student has ever had. Family and close friends are absent, along with the comfortable feeling of home and neighborhood. Even though these students like campus, they miss their family and their home more. This is homesickness.

Going to college isn't like going to summer camp. It's not going to be over in a week or two. This is a commitment that seems to stretch out endlessly before the homesick student. For students with strong cases of homesickness, often the best solution is to admit that college away from home *at this time of their lives* is a mistake.

If Elena had tried to handle this problem herself, she would never have withdrawn. Her grades would have gotten worse as the semester grew harder, and her frame of mind would have gotten worse with her grades. The college would have dropped her. She was in a can't-win situation.

Some problems are too large and too complicated for students to solve by themselves. That's why learning to talk to counselors and advisers is so important to your success as a student. Talking to an expert is the best way to go. **RU READY?**

Strategy 7

Studying vs. homework —
yes, there's a difference, a crucial one

Remember that idea of having a hole in your head that the teacher uncorks to fill your brain with knowledge? Wouldn't that be easy! Unfortunately, learning is not that simple. It takes energy, focus, and work. In fact, it's a process that goes beyond doing homework assignments. Doing homework assignments may have been good enough for grade school, but times have changed now that you're older, and you have to change with them.

Learn about yourself

Check all that apply.

How do you study?

_____ I study as hard as I feel like studying each night.

_____ The night before a big test, I really hit the books.

_____ I do every assignment that the teacher requires.

_____ I assume that if I do all the required assignments, I'll get an *A*.

_____ If I get in grade trouble, I do "extra-credit."

_____ I study "ahead" regularly, so I feel comfortable in each class.

_____ I know that for some subjects, I have to do more than homework.

_____ I don't have homework in every subject every night, so my study time varies each night.

_____ I study for every class every night.

_____ If a course is hard for me, I study harder for it.

_____ I usually don't work ahead on long-term assignments. I find I work better under the pressure of deadlines.

_____ I put my book under my pillow each night and hope that I gain information through osmosis.

_____ I believe staying alert in class each day will give me most of the knowledge I need.

Let's enter an imaginary classroom.

Class is ending, and the teacher reminds everyone that tomorrow, you're beginning a new chapter in the textbook. To get you and your classmates thinking about a certain concept in the chapter, the teacher gives a homework assignment: Write one page describing your opinion of that concept, a sort of first impression based on your reading.

It's the end of the school day, so you go home and start your homework, beginning with the course just mentioned. Starting a new chapter means reading new material. Okay, you start reading the chapter. Pretty soon, after you've read a few pages, you understand the concept you have to write about. So you begin writing.

Do you pull out your course notebook and start writing there? Or do you sit down at the computer to write your one-page assignment? Either way is good. After some time, you've filled a page with your thoughts. Your homework for that course is done… over… completed. Now you move on to the next assignment in another subject.

Stop a minute. Let's look more closely at what you're doing. If tomorrow you're going to start discussing a new chapter, you should read the *whole* chapter. Carefully. Read *AHEAD?* You say, "That's crazy!" No, it's not. You stopped reading as soon as you thought you knew enough to start writing. That raises a good question about studying. How much is enough? Is it enough to spend only the time it takes to complete the homework assignment for each subject? The answer is no. In this case, it's not enough just to begin reading the chapter and stop when you think you can fill a page with your impressions. Let's back up and create a better process.

Processing the information

As you start reading new material, you should be taking notes. Where? In your course notebook, naturally. Don't start highlighting anything in your textbook yet. Why? Because all this information is new — you'll end up highlighting everything. How much of the chapter can you read in an hour? And you shouldn't just read; you should be organizing information from the chapter in your notebook as you go.

At a certain point, you'll feel that you understand the concept you're supposed to write about. But are you sure you've got it? Maybe you'd better go back to the start of the chapter and reread. This second read should make everything clearer because the ideas are no longer brand-new to you. This time around, you can highlight more efficiently (and save some yellow ink) because you understand better what's really important.

Now you can start writing. But don't start composing quite yet. First, make some notes on a page or your computer screen. Rough out your thoughts. What are the basics of the concept? The teacher asked for an opinion. What is your opinion, and why?

First, explain the concept. Go back to your text and notes and do some quiet thinking. After you can explain the concept, you can start roughing out the second part, *"My personal opinion of this concept is…"* You finish the first draft and move on to studying another course. Later, you come back to the draft, and reread it for clarity, thoughtfulness, and accuracy. You also read for needed transitions, awkward phrasings, etc.

And don't forget a final proofreading, checking grammar, punctuation, and spelling. Look for missing words or extra words. DON'T depend on your word processor to find these kinds of mistakes.

Knowing the difference

Good grief! How in the world did we turn a simple homework assignment into such a big deal? You say, *"I could have completed that homework assignment quickly and easily: skim the first few pages of the chapter and dream up an opinion."* Yes, tomorrow you could turn in your paper, and then sit and listen to the teacher present the new chapter (sort of filling the hole in your head).

Or you could take the extra steps I suggested, really understand the material, write a better paper, and probably get a very high grade. Because you spent more time on the chapter, *the class becomes a review that increases your understanding of everything you've already read.* You know enough to ask good questions about unclear areas of the subject or to contribute to the class discussion.

In the first instance, you've completed your homework assignment the quick and easy way. In the second instance, you've completed your homework and STUDIED the subject. You've taken care to understand the concept, and you've written an intelligent paper.

Naturally, this learning process can be applied to problem-solving courses like math and science, too. For example, don't just plow through the problems assigned for math homework. Look at your textbook's explanation of new concepts. Notice how they compare with your teacher's presentation in class, and then review your work to be sure it's accurate.

There is a big difference between homework and study. You must understand the difference to really develop the study skills required in college.

The big difference

Let's set the record straight with a couple simple definitions:

> **Homework:** assignments given by a teacher, often to be handed in and graded.

> **Studying:** all the work you do to process and retain course information; *a self-directed, thorough effort.* The goal of studying is long-term learning. Long-term learning requires more than homework. (More on this in a few pages.)

The additional studying you do to complete assignments with precision and intelligence is very different from simple homework. Don't wait for the teachers to tell you to reread textbook material. Just know you must read material more than once if you want to understand it and *learn* it. Your job is to get the knowledge out of the book and into your memory. Some teachers don't "require" class notes. But most want you to take them, and then rewrite them at home to give you another level of understanding. This repetition of writing your notes again helps you remember concepts and details. The same applies to highlighting and outlining your textbooks. Repetition is crucial to your success.

As you understand more about studying, you'll learn to organize course material in special ways that makes learning easier *for you.* What works for someone else might not work for you. Class notes, outlines, flash cards, memory lists, rereading, reviewing, highlighting (on the second or later reading) is all part of the studying that successful students must do. I'll say it again because repeating things helps you remember them: Studying is very different from teacher-directed homework because you have to take the initiative to do it. Studying is a process. Some students think it's a single event — like cramming right before the test. That's wrong-headed.

The benefit of studying is a big one. When you study and prepare for class, the class itself becomes a form of studying! Because you're keeping up with the material, what the teacher talks about in class will make more sense to you — you've got the background information needed to follow along. Now you can ask intelligent questions or participate thoughtfully in the class discussion. Both are forms of studying because you are now actively involved in learning, not just sitting in class, passively listening to information for the first time. You're ready to learn. To borrow a phrase from sports, *"You've come to play."*

Why teachers give homework assignments

Homework is the traditional way teachers make sure that students are keeping up with their courses. In other words, teachers use homework assignments to make you work with course material. It's one way to judge if you are understanding and *learning* it. What's more, the practice of doing homework keeps your mind focused on the course, which means you'll understand new material as it's presented in class. If you know what's going on in class, you're more likely to participate. True, homework helps you learn, but learning doesn't end with homework.

You probably remember that in elementary school, and even middle school, doing a good job on homework usually guaranteed good, probably high, grades. But by high school, you should begin to notice that simply doing homework does not guarantee success. Why not?

As students progress in their education, teachers and courses become more demanding — they cover more and more material in less and less time. Therefore, *learning* begins to mean more than just doing assignments, reading chapters, writing papers, doing problems, etc. Students who earn consistently high grades in college (or high school) and fill their heads with long-term knowledge go above and beyond homework. They STUDY.

More about *studying*

As mentioned earlier, study takes an independent, self-directed effort — creating different methods to approach and learn different subjects. It involves doing extra work so you can do better — so you can learn long-term. This extra work can also raise your grade from a *B* to an *A*. What kinds of extra work?

- Studying is coming prepared for every class. You are up to date in your reading, and you have even read ahead. You have done all your practice exercises (even when they're not required), and you've gone over them.

- Studying is taking good notes in class and then carefully rewriting them later that day. You rewrite notes while information from class is still fresh in your mind, so you can add any details that you were too rushed to include during class. If you have a hard time keeping up with the teacher, bring a recorder to class. Ask the teacher if it's okay to record the class. Play back the class later in the day and take better notes at your own pace.

- Studying is not just doing the assigned reading, but *rereading* the material, and then taking notes and organizing what you've read by making flashcards, outlines, or lists.

- Studying is reviewing graded tests and assignments to really understand why you got an answer wrong, and figuring out how to prevent that mistake on the next test.

- Studying is starting a writing assignment ahead of time, so the paper can be roughed out at first and then rewritten and improved multiple times before you hand it in.

- Studying is doing a few extra problems in math and science "for practice" to make sure you really understand certain concepts and procedures. It keeps your skills sharp.

- Studying is rereading the notes from earlier in a course. It's a strategy that keeps the ideas of the *whole course* in your mind. Otherwise, you're learning only the current chapter and forgetting the earlier ones as you plow ahead.

- A few pages earlier, we said studying is reading and working *ahead* in all your courses. Let me repeat myself. Reading ahead gives you an edge and prevents confusion. When the teacher introduces a new theory or concept, you already know something about it. And if you *didn't* understand it when you read ahead, you can ask the teacher questions. If you *did* understand the material, then the teacher is *reviewing and clarifying for you* while only introducing the material to the other students. Reading ahead prevents bad starts and can give you great starts in learning new things. And it will help you contribute better to class discussions.

- Studying is going to your teacher when you have questions. And if you're really a college smart student, you frequently have questions. Having questions signals that you are involved in the learning process and your mind is developing from day to day.

- And, yes, studying is putting in that extra time right before big tests. But guess what? If you've been studying in all these other ways, on the night before a test, you'll only have to study minimally, which makes preparing for tests a whole lot less nerve-wracking.

Be college smart. So, technically speaking, when anyone asks, *"Do you have any homework tonight?"* your answer should always be *"yes."* There's always something you can "assign yourself." Studying always gives you an edge.

Big benefits of studying

1. *Excellent, not just good, grades.* **A** students who are always **A** students know that high grades come not just from doing homework but from studying, too.

2. *What you learn sticks with you.* Crammers can look pretty smart on their final grade reports. However, what they learned in a hurry is gone before they know it. And then when they move on to their next math or foreign-language course, they struggle to remember what they should have really learned already in earlier courses. When these students get to college, where the professor expects a foundation of knowledge or a certain skill, the crammers just won't have it. Then the trouble begins — and it never ends!

Is this the first time you've understood the difference between *homework* and *study?* If so, from now on, refer to all your schoolwork as *studying,* not *homework.* Just changing what you call your nightly efforts will remind you of your true focus: preparing for college.

Practice sharpens your skills.

If you haven't already done so, think of the learning you do each day in the same way you would prepare for an athletic event — you might lift weights, do stretching exercises, practice ball handling, etc. As we've said before, some people are gifted in athletics or the performing arts. You may be one. But on the court, the field, or the stage, those who are "the best" practice, work out, keep in shape, and stay serious about what they're doing. It's the same with learning. Gifted or not, if you practice (study), work out (study), keep in shape (study), and stay serious, you will get high grades. And just as importantly, *you'll remember what you learn,* so you have it to build on when you need it in college courses.

Students who have lost their grip

By the way, do you have any friends who fit the description below?

Many students think high school is "more school," not too much different than middle school. They do their homework, but they're not earning the grades that they used to. Why? They don't understand about studying. You've heard them in the halls. They blame the teacher: *"She doesn't like me." "His tests aren't fair."* Or they complain, saying, *"I'm not good in this subject."* Or they grumble, *"I'll never use this. Why do I need to know a foreign language, history, or physics? How's it going to help me?"* Depending on the student, almost any course can be declared "useless."

So once students come up with a good excuse for not doing well in a class, they have more or less given themselves permission to do mediocre work in it. After all, it's not their fault that the teacher doesn't like them, the subject is hard for them, or the information isn't useful for their particular lives. Trust me. That kind of thinking can hurt you badly.

There's an answer for each one of their excuses:

- *The teacher doesn't like me.* Teachers can't give high or low grades because they like or don't like you. Teachers have to be fair-minded in their grading and be able to defend their grades by evaluating everyone in the same way.
- *The tests aren't fair.* If students think the tests aren't fair, that probably means they simply haven't studied enough to be able to answer the questions. Or maybe their minds were somewhere else when the teacher talked about what material would be covered on the upcoming test.
- *The subject is too hard for me.* Remember that things get harder as your education progresses. Don't play the victim. Have you ever noticed that a kid who won't study harder as the course gets harder may play a video game for hours to improve a personal score? Funny, don't you think?
- *This course is useless.* If a student thinks the course is useless, that's just his or her opinion. The student is not yet old enough to understand how all the things you learn come together to form the mind of a college student or a thinking adult.

About that last point. You get a double benefit from every course you take. The first benefit is obvious: You gain knowledge you probably didn't have before. The second benefit is even more important: The course makes you think in new ways. Every course forces you to develop different thinking skills that affect the growth of your mind. This is an important fact, but few students understand it. The next section explains why all courses are important.

Why everything's important

Many former students with successful careers come back to visit and tell me how important one course or another has been to them, *although they didn't know it at the time.* They say that these courses gave them knowledge or special thinking skills that are essential to their work now.

Think about this: the way you learn mathematics is different from the way you learn history, which is different from the way you learn literature. All of these courses give you a different kind of mental exercise and skills. You don't know what the future holds for you — in college or in the workplace — which means that every course you take is important.

If you have a mind that can think and learn in a whole variety of ways, your future will be filled with a variety of career opportunities. Once you start saying that *"this course is dumb"* or that course is *"worthless,"* you begin closing doors to your future, one after another. Close your mind to your education, and you close your mind to life opportunities.

Finally, all your courses are important for another, more immediate reason. School, like sports, is competitive, and there may be only so many seats available in the freshman class of the colleges you are interested in. You're competing for a seat, just like you compete for a place on a team. Studying all of your courses will give you a competitive edge. Keep working on these Strategies!

Plagiarism — handing in someone else's work

Imagine that you work long and hard on a 10-page research paper on George Washington for your American History course. You get an *A+*. What a feeling of accomplishment!

Then, next semester, you find out that, without your knowing it, another student has gotten your paper and used your hard work for an assignment in American Politics. *How would you feel?* Would you feel betrayed, cheated, "robbed?"

Yes! While you weren't robbed of money or other valuables, your thoughts, your time, and your hard work were stolen. The other student is guilty of a type of academic cheating called *plagiarism.*

Plagiarism is taking someone else's thoughts and words and using them as your own.

In our example, it doesn't matter how your *A+* paper was used. The student might have turned in your entire paper with his or her name on it. Maybe the student used only part of your work for a shorter assignment — or "spoke" your paper for an oral report on the first U.S. president.

What if the other student didn't use your words exactly — just used your thoughts and analysis? It doesn't make any difference. If your paper was used by someone else in any way without your permission, it is still plagiarism.

A more likely example. Plagiarism, of course, does not usually occur between students. It occurs when a student has an assignment to write (or talk about) and then reads (researches) what other people have written about the subject. When the student uses the words or thoughts of someone else without giving credit to the source of the information (as in footnotes), it's plagiarism.

Plagiarism occurs whether the information comes out of a published book with an author's name on it or comes from the Internet without a person's name connected to it. If you use words and thoughts that are not yours — either directly or indirectly — you have to include your source.

Let's say you're writing a short essay. If you read other sources (even as simple as an encyclopedia) and use ideas and information you found there, you have to mention that source.

Colleges expect that you understand plagiarism. So learn the rules of using sources right now. Being caught plagiarizing always involves a penalty. A college penalty can be devastating because you might be asked to leave the school, and your plagiarism can go on your permanent record.

Internet services. Internet "services" will write papers for students to turn in as their own work. These services cover themselves by saying you shouldn't turn in their work as homework assignments. True, Internet sites warn about cheating and plagiarism. But if they were really worried about such things, they wouldn't exist, and they wouldn't take the money of dishonest students.

You can't do anything about Internet Cheating Services because they hide behind the First Amendment. But remember this: Every student who cheats is cheating you as well as all the other students who honestly do their own work. Plagiarists lower the standards of the school.

Combating plagiarism. Just as students use the Internet to cheat, teachers are using the Internet to discover when plagiarism is occurring, so more and more cases of "Internet plagiarism" are being "caught."

As an honest student, you should understand what plagiarism is, and don't do it. Don't do it, because you cheat yourself and your education. Don't do it, because you're cheating others. And don't do it, because it's dangerous. If you plagiarize and get caught, it's something that can follow you for the rest of your life.

Listen to Dr. Bob —

Why you need to practice this Strategy for college

I've told you this before, and I'll say it again. It's important enough to repeat many times. One of the biggest mistakes that college students make is to think that college is going to be like high school, only away from home. It's not. It's very different. What else do you need to remember?

- College instructors pack much more content in a semester than teachers in high school.

- College semesters are shorter; their pace is faster than you can imagine right now.

- Tests are far fewer in college, so every test counts more, and low test grades turn into low final grades. (Remember: There's no "extra credit" to bring those grades up.)

- Professors do not usually give "homework assignments," only reading assignments.

- You are expected to learn independently outside of class.

- You are supposed to study 2-3 hours for each hour you spend in class.

In college, a course may meet only 3 times a week. That means you spend only 15 to 20 hours in class each week — not much compared to the almost 40 hours a week you're in class now. During class time, college instructors present only a small amount of the material to be covered in the course. The rest is up to you.

Having all that unscheduled time outside of class means that you can choose when and if to study. Some students don't get it. They think to themselves, *Wow! I have all this time. I can do anything I want!* No, they can't. They are in college TO STUDY. That's their "job."

That freedom to choose is particularly dangerous for some college students addicted to certain distracting activities. These students abuse their freedom and damage their grades so badly that they have to quit school or are asked to leave. What kind of addictions am I talking about? Playing video games, emailing, watching TV, talking on the phone, playing cards, staying up half the night talking to friends — or worse, partying several nights a week.

If you think "addiction" is too strong a word, you're wrong. We know that drinking and drugs can be addictive, but students who spend 25 hours a week on email or get/send 100 phone calls a day have a serious problem, too. I once met a student, a video gamer who played games 19 hours a day. He didn't go to class. He didn't sleep much. He also denied that he had a problem. People with addictions always do.

I've met these students. They devote all their time and energy to satisfying their addictions. They are out of control. Start now to learn how to balance your freedom with your responsibility to your future.

Earlier in this guidebook you discovered how full your days are. You have lots of non-school activities going on, and it's tempting to push studying off to the side to do other things. You can't cave in like that. If you don't control your time so that you balance studying with activities, you create problems for yourself. On the other hand, if you are self-reliant and study productively, you'll have time for all the things you want to do.

Do you remember Strategy 1? We talked about using your brain as a processor. You "process" information by using the tactics described in this Strategy — working with the material until it's firmly in your head. Studying is working at learning the same way you work at sport skills or playing an instrument. You repeat and repeat and repeat. Practice, practice, practice to win!

PSST! If at times you say to yourself, *"These strategies take effort. Why can't my life be easy?"* Answer yourself by saying, *"My education is one of the most important things in my life."* College demands a lot, but it's also the key that opens doors and opportunities for the rest of your life. So be college smart and apply yourself. The harder you work now, the more successful you'll be in college and in your career. Go back and carefully read all the bullets and lists.

Up close and personal
Marcus: A bright guy, but a slow learner

Marcus had always been a top student in high school and never had any problems. Now, in his fourth college semester, he was afraid he was going to lose his merit scholarship and his place in the honors program. His grades had been sliding since his freshman year. Marcus had come to see me this semester because although he had been an *A*-student in high school, he had slid into the *B*-range in most of his college courses.

Marcus complained, *"I'm doing the same thing now that I did in high school, when I got As. I don't get it."* As I looked at Marcus's high school transcript, I saw that he had earned only two *B*s during his entire high school career, one in Advanced Chemistry and one in an Advanced Placement American History course. When I asked Marcus why he hadn't earned *A*s in those courses, too, he told me that the teachers had given "really hard" tests.

Marcus's ACT scores were in the 30s. Why couldn't he get an *A* in those two courses? Marcus didn't know. With his intelligence, this was an important question.

I asked Marcus how he prepared for tests. He told me that he went to class every day, listened carefully, did the homework, and studied hard the night before a test. He was a crammer — that got him through high school with *A*s.

Correction: That *usually* earned him *A*s. Remember — he didn't earn *A*s in Advanced Chemistry and AP History. He couldn't get past a *B*. Why? Marcus was a Typical Student. He studied irregularly. When he crammed, the good grades he received gave him the illusion that he was learning. But he didn't study enough to earn *A*s in tough courses.

The *B*s were trying to tell him something, and being a Typical Student, he'd missed the point. When courses get harder, you must study harder *to maintain A grades*. And that's why he was in trouble now.

His college classes had gotten harder with every passing semester. He couldn't see that his old routine wasn't working — even though he'd had four semesters of low grades staring him in the face. He still clung stubbornly to his old routine, hoping that "next time," things would work out all right.

Quite simply, he wasn't doing enough. He needed to give his courses more energy and more time.

Since he couldn't evaluate his situation, I helped him. I introduced Marcus to the idea that studying for tests is actually an everyday process — from Day One of each semester and in every course. True, most tests still require some extra study time, a few days before the test, to review to make sure that all the course material is still there at your fingertips.

As we talked, Marcus admitted that the only time he spent on courses outside of class was doing homework assignments. That's not anywhere near enough. In college, instructors expect you to study without assigning you work. Simply doing "homework" assignments will not put you in control of your courses.

Anybody can say a teacher gives hard or tricky tests, but if you know the material, that shouldn't matter. The fact is that Marcus got *B*s and *C*s because he didn't know how to study. He didn't know the material *well enough*. To save his scholarship, he had to really study and learn, not just do assignments.

Dean's commentary

At the beginning of our conversation, Marcus said to me, *"I'm doing the same thing now that I did in high school, when I got As. I don't get it."* I wanted to tell Marcus what students forget: College is harder than high school, so test-prep techniques that earned *A*s in high school might only earn *B*s (if that) in college. I didn't give him this answer because I thought there might be more to Marcus's story than that. There wasn't. It was so simple. He just couldn't see it.

Marcus's solution was to study every day. That's the way to prepare for tests. You build a bank of knowledge a little at a time and add to it every day. Because you keep up with your work, you understand classroom presentations better, which makes the work you do outside of class easier and more meaningful.

Marcus had already proven that simply going to class, listening, doing assignments, and studying the night before the test didn't work anymore. His ACT scores told him he had the ability to succeed. However, if he didn't alter what he'd been doing, no dramatic change would take place.

Two changes had already taken place: He knew that he could no longer continue to say that his low grades were a mystery to him. Neither could he blame the teacher for being "hard." Professors are supposed to be harder: This is college.

If Marcus had continued to blame his professors for his falling grades, he would never have figured out how to succeed in school — or in life. When students say that tests are too hard, that's usually just an excuse. What's really going on? They still haven't accepted the fact that **learning takes time. RU READY?**

Strategy 8

Creating a schedule (ugh!) —
getting control of your life (finally!)

How often have you felt like you have so many things to do you can't possibly get them all done? There's no question that students are busy people — so busy that they often feel pressed for time, stressed out, and overwhelmed. What about you? Do you control your days, or do they control you? Do you find yourself robbing time from one thing to make room for another? Do you let things go unfinished, hoping it won't make any difference? Do you keep your fingers crossed that those pages you didn't have time to study won't be on the test? Do you wish for luck — that you'll get "an easy grade" on an assignment you did at the last minute? Do you find it hard to fit in homework and study? (Don't forget you have to do both!) Stressful, isn't it?

If you answered yes to any of these questions, you need a personal schedule, a map to follow each day to organize your life and really become college smart. Creating a schedule is one of the most important things you can do for yourself. Scheduling not only will get you into a good college, but it is a skill that will enable you to graduate from college! (Plus, you'll graduate on time and with a major area of study and a degree you really want.)

Freedom or anarchy?

The thought of making a schedule, much less sticking to it, makes a lot of students cringe. Why? Schedules seem to take away freedom. When you HAVE to do things at certain times on certain days, you might feel that your independence has just flown out the window. But the truth of the matter is that following a schedule is one of the most freeing (yes, FREEING) things you can do. No matter how complicated and busy you may be, a schedule will make your life a lot easier, more comfortable, and more enjoyable. And on top of it all, you'll have a great feeling of accomplishment.

> **Be college smart.** Schedules give you enough time to do the many things in your hectic life without the usual stress or worries. Developing even a simple schedule can be a very invigorating experience for a student. Try it. Schedules definitely take away that awful feeling of *"I can't possibly do everything I'm supposed to do."*

Mapping out a schedule is a mark of a mature student, and it's a skill you'll need for college. A schedule and a college smart attitude toward studying can keep you on top academically at all times — no matter how demanding your courses or your days may be.

Learn about yourself

Remember how you mapped out time for all of your activities in **The person inside the student** chapter? Go back and look at it now. When you worked out that Activity Map, you didn't understand as much about being a student as you do now. At this point, you have a better idea of how to use your time and roughly how many activities *reasonably* fit into an average week. You know your many roles and responsibilities, and you've probably also come to see that some are more important than others. This Strategy and the ones that follow will help you under-stand the value of organizing the various responsibilities of your life.

And now that you've learned the difference between homework and study, making a personal schedule for yourself is a sign that you are moving away from the overly simple learning habits of a child toward the more mature learning behavior of a college smart student.

Before we actually create a personal schedule, let's analyze carefully everything you do in a typical day. To do this, use the chart on page 125, which is a larger version of the chart below. Choose a single day on the chart, and record everything you do before and after school: starting at 7:00 a.m. and ending at 11:00 p.m. Be as specific as you can. It will be like keeping an hour-by-hour diary of your day.

As you fill in your day —

- Write in all the things you do outside of school: lessons, meal times, athletic practices, part-time job, household chores, hanging out with friends (in person or by phone or by computer), watching TV and listening to music, and, of course, homework and studying.

- In a given hour, you probably do several things. List them all.

- Be careful and accurate.

The purpose of this exercise is to get you to look closely at a single day to see all the things you do, *and* to see how much time you devote to school work OUTSIDE of your school day. Now go to page 125 and, working with a pencil, so you can erase as you think through your day, fill in one day of **My Week in Review**.

	Sun	Mon	Tue	Wed	Thu	Fri	Sat
7:00							
8:00							
9:00							
10:00							
11:00							
12:00							
1:00							
2:00							
3:00							
4:00							
5:00							
6:00							
7:00							
8:00							
9:00							
10:00							
11:00	Go to Bed!	Go to Bed!	Go to Bed!	Go to Bed!	Go to Bed!	Go to Bed!	Go to Bed!

When you've finished your "diary for a day," look at the time you give to homework and study. Do you spend more or less time than you thought? At the end of the day, if you go to bed feeling you've accomplished a lot and you're satisfied with your life as a student in general, you've probably got your life organized already. You might not need scheduling advice.

On the other hand, if you go to bed later than you should, wondering if tomorrow you'll be able to work around the studying and assignments you haven't completed… if the thought of tomorrow means you'll have to face even more things you might not have time to finish, then you need advice about creating a **Personal Study Schedule**. Your new organized life is right around the corner. Get ready — we're about to get you scheduled!

Step 1 — Finding the time

Continue filling out **My Week in Review** — but as you fill in the rest of the days, keep these points in mind:

Blocking out. See how your time is already blocked out while you're in school? Those hours are not available to you for study. For now, though, these times don't count. What other activities in your days prevent you from studying during certain hours? Do you play a sport? Take music lessons? Are you in a club or organization that meets regularly? Do you work a part-time job? Block out those hours, too, because you cannot control them.

For now, cross off your weekend from Friday night to Sunday afternoon. You may occasionally have to study on weekends, but for now you're creating a basic study schedule.

Identifying free time. After you have blocked out the hours that are not available for study time, take a moment to notice how many hours on your schedule sheet are actually available.

Looking for empty blocks. After-school time is great for studying because your mind is already in a learning mode from a day of being in class. After a snack, you could get in some good blocks of study before dinner. Obviously, if you have after-school conflicts, your study schedule might not start until after dinner. The time from 7:00 p.m. to bedtime — which should be no later than 11:00 o'clock — gives you four hours during which you can schedule longer, uninterrupted periods of study.

Adding up hours. So from Sunday evening (you have to get ready for Monday classes) through Thursday evening, you have five nights of at least four hours each night to study. That's 20 hours. And if you get home right after school, you can add two more hours each day. How many hours is that? 30 hours.

Great! You have 30 hours each week from which to choose study time! You have a lot more opportunity for scheduled study than you think. Yes, you may even do some studying during your school days — in a study period or during lunchtime.

Where the time goes. Right now, much of that non-school time is filled with your personal interests and activities like TV, being with friends, chatting on the phone or online, listening to music, playing computer games and, just being with your family. That means you are often trying to work in occasional bits of study time between all these other things.

Organize your thinking. Creating a workable and productive personal schedule for yourself begins with recognizing several facts.

1. You're a busy person who does many different things — most are haphazard and unscheduled.

2. Your best times to study are after school and in the evening hours.

3. As a college smart student, you need to develop your learning skills by doing homework AND studying.

4. You'll have to move some of your less-important activities out of the way to make room for regular study time.

Think of your life at this moment like a table full of clutter. For many high school students, this comparison is exactly right. You have to push the clutter out of the way to make room for more important things — in this case, things having to do with studying and learning. Studying comes first. Clutter comes second. Yes, clutter can be fun, but colleges won't be interested in you because you have an amazing collection of clutter.

Want some examples of clutter?

- Video games
- Phones
- Chatting online
- Surfing the Web
- Watching TV and movies

- Hanging out with friends
- Going to the mall
- Listening to music
- Surfing, online gaming, & profiling sites
- Napping because you stay up too late

Did you know that the Kaiser Family Foundation (a group that studies how kids 8-18 use their time) found that today's students can spend 3.5 to 5 hours a day just on games and TV! When you add all the other clutter, you are really eating up study time.

Be determined to get your priorities straight, and in this case, that means identifying those times of your day when being a student becomes more important than clutter. It's the time when you do homework assignments, read and organize your class notes and textbook materials, keep ahead of your class outlines, write and rewrite papers, and prepare for tests. In other words, next to class time, your personal study time is the most important time of your week. Set aside blocks of time, study efficiently, and *then* build in time for other things, like entertainment.

Step 2 — How many hours?

You're trying to get ready for college. As a college freshman, you should be studying at least 30 hours each week. You should work up to that number gradually over your four years of high school. Look at the hours listed in the following chart. It shows the recommended number of study hours a week for each year of high school.

Year of School	Minimum Number of Study Hours Each Week
Freshman Year	10 hours
Sophomore Year	15 hours
Junior Year	20 hours
Senior Year	25 hours

Some students with heavy course loads may very well have to study more than the number of recommended hours. But to prepare yourself for college, you should not be studying fewer hours than the chart recommends. As you look at **My Week in Review**, can you find the number of hours you need? If not, you must eliminate some clutter.

Each of the totals in the chart above represents the number of hours you have to divide among your courses. You should spend as many hours on each course as needed to achieve the highest grades possible. How do you decide? That's the next step. For now, just accept this warning. Even if you are doing very well in your classes, resist the temptation to decrease the number of hours in the chart. Courses naturally get harder as the semester progresses because there is more and more complicated course material to deal with. Keep this in mind: You're spending your scheduled study time *to really learn,* not just cram for the next test.

The backbone of all 12 Strategies: putting in the time

Now that you are evolving as a college smart student who understands the need for long-term learning, the following words will hold even more meaning for you.

No matter what your high school grades are now, you have to develop the skill of scheduling your time to really learn. NOT developing this habit is one of the major reasons that one out of every four college freshmen fails to return to campus sophomore year. Only one in three college students graduates in four years. These are awful statistics. Make sure NOW that you don't become one of them.

Don't forget that *learning is your full-time job.* In college, you can expect to study at least 30 hours a week as a freshman. These are hours *on top* of your in-class hours. This number will grow a few hours with each passing year in college. Let's concentrate on what you need to do *now* to get you in shape to handle those hours.

Step 3 — Dividing time among your courses

Once you know how many hours you should be studying each week, then you must decide how much time you should spend on each of your courses. Discovering "how much" is the only tricky part of creating your **Personal Study Schedule**. But after you do it once, you'll be able to do it automatically in later semesters. It's like riding a bike — you won't forget how.

In an ideal world, each of your courses would require the same amount of homework and study time. You could simply divide your total time by the number of courses you are taking. But unfortunately, there is nothing ideal about your school life.

- Different courses and teachers require different amounts of study time.

- You will find some courses harder than others, so you have to spend more time on them.

- Harder courses stay harder throughout the semester, and even easy courses get harder as the semester moves on.

Remember the Strategy called **The first two weeks**? It explained how you should use the first two weeks of the semester to pay careful attention in all your courses, so you can get off to a strong start. Well, it's during these first two weeks that you will discover the difficulty of your various courses. This is your trial period. You'll be figuring out how much time you need to do a good job of learning for each course.

By the end of the first two weeks, you should be able to list your courses from the most difficult to the least challenging. That's the order you should use when you study. As you assign homework and study time in your **Personal Study Schedule**, arrange the order of your courses so you study your most difficult courses first and your easiest course last.

Let's say you're a sophomore, so you should be studying 15 to 20 hours each week. If you cannot schedule any homework and study hours after school, you must use the hours from 7:00 p.m. to 11 p.m. There are pluses and minuses to this situation. The non-study activities that fill your time after school give you "break" time to do non-academic activities, like sports and clubs. Taking a break in midday can be good, but understand that these activities mean that ALL your study hours are now pushed into the evening. Can you see why being on major athletic teams *all year long,* working part-time during the week, or joining too many clubs can complicate your day? They add pressure and demand good organization. As long as you use a **Personal Study Schedule**, though, you'll be able to manage the load.

After you've earned a few test grades early in the semester, you'll know how your study effort is paying off, and you can give just the right amount of time to each of your courses. Then you'll know how to divide up your study hours according the difficulty of your courses. As you move through the semester, you'll learn how to adjust your hours to match your ability and the pace that you study. You'll be in control. And being in control will reduce your stress and make you feel better about yourself and your days.

A caution: Remember that discovering how many hours must be applied to each course does not mean figuring out how *little* you need to study. No. You start out with a total minimum number of hours to study (follow the chart of hours for each year of high school). Then divide that total into amounts needed for each of your courses from hardest to easiest. The more hours you study, the better you will do. Keep in mind that study is not only a process of gaining knowledge but also an exercise in developing all the parts of your mind. Knowledge may eventually fade from memory as years go by, but a well-developed mind stays with you forever.

Other essentials

In creating a workable **Personal Study Schedule**, you have to push less-important things in your life aside, like sweeping the clutter off a table. But you also have essential non-school activities in your life that must be given time within your study schedule. You may have family and home responsibilities. Or you may have a part-time job. They are important, but they need to be scheduled just like your studies.

When you create your first **Personal Study Schedule**, get your parents involved. Let them know what you're doing to gear up for college. They might be able to help you move the time of your music lessons so they don't sit in the middle of a block of study time. You need your parents' help in other ways, too. You don't want to neglect home chores, but while you're studying, you can't be doing other things, like looking after your little brother or sister. As you schedule study blocks, you'll have to be aware of your other roles and plan accordingly with your parents to protect your study time.

Once you've found and blocked out the number of study hours you need on **My Week in Review,** you're ready to start planning out your **Personal Study Schedule**. Read the rest of the Strategy for more points before you start working on your Schedule on page 126.

Some tips on schedules

Keep these details in mind as you make your new **Personal Study Schedule**. Review them often.

- Be patient. It takes time to adjust from being a "scattered" student to an organized one. After a week or two, you'll regret that you haven't been using a schedule long before. Really! Being in control is a great feeling.

- Make your **Personal Study Schedule** *simple* and easy to follow. Students give up on complicated schedules that change all the time and are hard to follow.

- Try to study the same courses at the same time. Your mind likes that routine. And regularity increases your study efficiency.

- Assign some time to each course each day. Don't ignore or disregard your "easier" courses. By neglecting these courses, you lose the balance of knowledge among your courses.

- Ask teachers, *"How long should I study each night to keep pace with this course?"*

- Studying for all your courses each day will give you a feeling of great accomplishment every day.

- Big tests and big assignments coming due? You should work on those in advance, maybe adding to your regular study time if you need to.

- *Never* cancel your regular study time to cram for a test.

- The more challenging the course, the more time is required.

- If your study schedule gets interrupted, be sure to make up the lost time.

- Schedule short "study breaks" for yourself. Exercise, read a magazine, turn on some music, eat a snack. Don't get involved in something like a phone call or TV show that will pull you away from your schedule for too long a time.

- Always give yourself enough time to eat, sleep, and exercise. Ignoring your health will get you in trouble sooner or later.

Scheduling vs. the glass wall

Your friends might prefer to study only when they have to. It's a strategy that will hurl them into what I call the *academic glass wall* sooner or later. What's that? It means coming to an abrupt stop and not being able to see the obstacle in front of your face.

Here are the symptoms. It's harder to understand the material your teacher presents in class. You always feel behind. You can't believe it when tests occur so quickly one after the other. You're always trying to find excuses for low grades and late assignments. It seems that teachers don't like you. You wonder if successful students know some secret that they're keeping from you. Grades go up and down, or drop altogether. Maybe your brain has been suddenly sucked dry by aliens!

No, there aren't any aliens involved. The problem is that you've hit it. WHAM!! Hit what?

The academic glass wall, the result of haphazard and unscheduled study time. Everything seemed okay before, but now your academic life has changed. Students who hit the wall are just not studying enough to keep up with courses that are getting harder and more demanding. Unscheduled and haphazard studying doesn't work anymore.

Schedules help control the variables.

But, you might argue, *grades still depend on the course or on the teacher.* True. Some courses are harder than others. Just like some teachers. But that's just the point. There are so many variables involved in getting good grades —

- the difficulty of the course
- the demands of the teacher
- the kinds of tests and assignments given
- how good you are in a subject
- how many other things you have going on in your life
- how committed you are to doing well

So many variables. And you've got to *control* them. When we talk about getting control of your life and your courses, we're really talking about following a **Personal Study Schedule**. You can have a great study place, and you can understand what it means to study, but if you cannot build into your day the TIME to study, nothing happens. Strategy 12 will tell you about the great number of students who never graduate from college. Making room for daily study time and using it productively is the #1 downfall of these students.

Starting now, take control of your days. You are the only one who can. (Adults call this *time management*.) Think of it this way:

- **Your schedule is a defense.** It prevents the nonessential things in your life from getting between you and learning, between you and the time-management skills you need for college.
- **Your schedule is an offense.** It gives you the means to adjust to tough teachers and tough subjects.

- **Your schedule is a fence.** A schedule ropes off time. Because blocks of time are separate, marked for distinct purposes, you are able to do more things, both study and leisure.
- **Your schedule is a stress-reliever.** It prevents you from being a scrambler who's always feeling behind, stressed, and dodging one school-related bullet after another.

Be college smart. Never mind about the grades you have typically received in the past. Look at the future. In high school and college, sharp learning skills (and the high grades that follow) are the product of time spent studying. Schedule your study hours — plan them out and write them down, preferably on a schedule sheet. Your schedule is your best defense against low grades and your virtual guarantee of high ones. This is a truth, so let it sink deep into your brain and don't forget it. *You'll find a blank schedule at the end of this Strategy. Make photocopies and USE them.*

What experienced teachers say

Teachers who really pay attention to the learning habits of their students all say the same things:

- Students who study regularly get the highest grades.
- Students who increase their study hours from year to year get the highest grades.
- Students who study more hours than "the minimum" each week get the highest grades.

Students who get *A*s study more each year of their education. And whether or not you want to admit it, next year will be harder than this year. College will be harder than high school. Get ready now. Don't learn it the hard way. Mistakes now will affect your future.

College students who always get high grades, enjoy their courses, and reach their goals are also the students who develop and stick to a schedule at the start of every semester. Schedules can turn your life around. Even students in deep academic trouble improve their lives dramatically when they adopt **Personal Study Schedules**. I've seen it happen again and again.

Part-time jobs

And then there's the matter of part-time jobs. Many students work too many hours. They often find their work hours increase just when tests occur and papers are due. True, everybody can use more money, especially students saving for college. But at what cost? If your grades suffer because you work too many hours, you are jeopardizing your college future, which is your doorway to a career.

The National Institute for Work and Learning in Washington, DC, recommends that in high school, you work only 10 hours a week during the school year — with the majority of those hours falling on the weekend. (If you need more money, work during the summers!)

Research shows that when high school students work 15 or more hours a week, grades fall and standardized test scores fall. Do you know what else? Students take less-demanding courses so they have more time to work their jobs. Bad decision. The real money lies not in flipping burgers, but in getting a high school education that colleges usually reward with generous financial-aid scholarships and grants.

Money now or later?

There's also another caution about part-time jobs. Ever heard the term *delayed gratification?* It refers to controlling yourself, not always getting what you want when you want it. Instead of buying a new cell phone as soon as the new model comes out, you wait for a sale. Rather than buying the latest computer game when it hits the stores, you wait for your birthday to roll around (and drop a lot of hints the week before).

Some students with part-time jobs have a problem with delayed gratification. The money they earn is quickly spent. They might say they're "saving for college," but, in truth, few dollars end up in a college savings account.

Earning and immediately spending too much money is the downfall of many students. They work more and more hours because they want more and more money to spend. In the end, they don't have time or energy to study.

I've known high school students who have become very used to making lots of money and spending it. When they get to college and they're on their own, they spend even more. Therefore, they work even more hours. As a result, their grades fall. They drop out of college and don't return. They say college was "just not for them." Translation: They can't live without a large income to satisfy their need for personal comforts.

They'll tell you, *"I'm making good money, and I expect to be a manger of the store where I work."* What really happens? They quickly reach a career plateau, and by the time they're 30 years old, they're making about as much as they will for the rest of their lives.

 Be college smart. Make studies your first priority. Working a reasonable number of hours at a part-time job is good experience — you can mention it on your college application. But working too much will affect the grades on your high school transcript. Colleges are very familiar with students who work for money more than they study for grades. These are students who need extra years to graduate or never graduate at all. Think about earning your spending money by going "all out" in your summer job.

 Listen to Dr. Bob —

Why you need to practice this Strategy for college

Of all the 12 Strategies that I want you to develop and use, scheduling is one of the most important.

You must become an independent student who controls your learning and your days. Scheduling helps you do both. Remember the idea of productivity? It's one of the biggest problems that college students face. They *waste all that "free time"* when they're not in class. Students don't get it. It isn't "free" time. It's unscheduled time. Their instructors expect them to be using that time to study. But the students are using that time to hang out, play video games, talk with their friends, or turn dorm life into a never-ending party. Suddenly, "all that time" just disappears.

They find themselves facing a major test or a project deadline, and they're scrambling. They're behind, and they don't know why.

Here's why: They had so much time that they didn't know how to control it. They didn't have the will power or the organization. They needed some structure, and no one was around telling them what to do. They lost sight of the fact that they could have balanced being productive and having fun. Now they're in trouble in their classes. They may have to drop a class. They don't have high enough grades to stay in their area of study. Some students lose their dreams because they cannot control their lives.

Schedules help you control your life. In fact, the more time you want to be free to do the things you want to do, the more control you must have over your life by managing your time.

Scheduling is like planning a well-organized study place for yourself. If you don't have a workable study place, you can't even begin to study. And if you don't have a workable **Personal Study Schedule**, you won't study enough to really learn the material in your high school courses and prepare yourself for college.

Let's recall the idea of comparing your education to climbing a mountain. As you move up the mountain of education, your courses become more challenging, and learning makes greater demands on your mind and your time. If you you don't develop more mature study skills, you will never make progress up the mountain. At best, you will simply move *around* the

How to make REALLY BIG money

All college students can get financial aid to help pay for the high costs of college — tuition, fees, room, and board. One form of financial aid is called *merit-based*. It comes in the form of scholarships and grants.

Merit-based dollars are awarded to excellent, well-rounded students who earn high grades *in challenging courses* and high scores on ACT and SAT tests.

Here's the big deal. **These are not loans. They do not have to be paid back.** They are given to students who have worked very hard in high school and have achieved great success because of their effort. Colleges want these students and are willing to pay part of college costs to attract these students to campus.

With a merit-based scholarship, you could earn thousands of dollars. This money is every bit as important as your parents starting a college-savings plan when you were in kindergarten.

So hang a little note above your study place that reads *High Grades and Test Scores Equal Big $$$$$ for College.*

Get college smart. If you give study a high priority now, you won't still be paying off your college loans when your own kids go off to college.

mountain, but at the same elevation. So be college smart and move up your particular mountain with energy, determination, courage, and your **Personal Study Schedule**.

Take the advice of all the people who are willing to help you on your educational expedition. But keep in mind that you are the one who is responsible for your success and your failure. Keep a positive outlook, set your goals clearly, work hard, and you'll reach that summit and see a view of the wonderful life you have ahead of you.

 PSST! Read through the highlighted passages. They summarize why scheduling reduces stress, increases your free time, and boosts your grades! What could be better than that? Start filling out the practice schedule right now, so you can see that you have plenty of time to do what you want and need to do.

Up close and personal
Liza: Misplaced priorities changed her future.

Liza was a freshman living off campus (at home) who came to me because her father insisted that she see someone about her academic difficulties. She thought that meant she could spend the time with me complaining about her low grades.

After midterms, she was getting *C*s and low *B*s in all her courses. She had gotten *A*s all through high school. She loved being at the university, she liked her courses, and she had decided on a major: psychology. She wanted to be a psychologist, a counselor who helps people. But she was sitting in my office to say that she didn't deserve such low grades.

I asked her if she thought that any of these grades were assigned in error. She said no — her test grades warranted the midterm grades she got. To Liza, the larger issue was that college teachers were unreasonable. They expected too much. If she used her time the way they wanted her to, she didn't have any time for a life. I said that she should tell me about it, and together we would try to figure out a solution.

To identify the problem, I began as I often do, by asking Liza to fill out a blank schedule sheet to show me how she used her time. She half-heartedly tried to fit in study time in the evenings Sunday through Thursday. She wasn't putting in any study time on the weekends. Instead, she slept late and then worked from noon to 6:00 p.m. on Saturday and Sunday. After work, she hung out with old high school friends who lived in the city. I asked Liza what kind of job she worked. She said that she waited tables, and the money was good. I asked if she needed the money. She said no. She just liked having lots of spending money for clothes.

I pointed out to her that the way she was spending her weekends caused her to lose two of the seven days in her week. She told me that work (and buying clothes) was important to her, and so were her old friends. She didn't get to see her high school friends during the week, so she had to use the weekends to do that. She felt that weekends were supposed to be "time off" — time to do what she wanted and unwind from a week of classes.

Then I examined Monday through Friday more closely and saw that Liza wasn't studying much outside of class. I asked her several more questions, but she was avoiding something. Eventually, it came out that she also worked five hours on Tuesday night until 11:00. By the time she got home, it was midnight. She woke up Wednesday tired – both physically and mentally. She had three classes on Wednesday, two of them in the morning.

We talked for a while about how being a server in a restaurant is a physically demanding job, more so than being a salesperson, a receptionist, or a file clerk. I was trying to get Liza to realize that she was devoting three days of her seven-day week to hard physical work. It was eating away her time, exhausting her, and affecting her school performance. No wonder she felt that she "deserved" free time. *Liza's tiredness wasn't coming from classes and studying, but from her job.*

I asked her what would happen if she spent an additional five hours — the length of her Tuesday work shift — on any one of her courses. She very reluctantly admitted that her grades would probably improve. But Liza would not yield. She dug in her heels and said that her weekends ought to be hers to use the way she wanted to. And no, she wouldn't give up her Tuesday hours, either. She wanted the money.

I told her that there would be consequences later on if she didn't improve her grades. She would never become a counselor. She thought I was wrong, and she would worry about that later.

Several semesters passed, and Liza's father made several appointments to see me and asked Liza to attend the meetings. He was worried about Liza's progress. Her grades continued to be average. I explained the problem to him. Until Liza let go of her feeling of being "entitled" to her weekend free time and until money became less important to her, she would not change. Her 2.7 grade point average was not going to prevent her graduation, but it would prevent her from pursuing a career as a counselor.

During those meetings, Liza's dad and I both tried to persuade her that her ideas about what she "deserved" were very different from the way the world worked. Her father knew that her grades were not going to get Liza where she wanted to go. She didn't believe either of us.

The point was driven home to Liza in the fall of her senior year. To become a psychologist, Liza had to go on to graduate school. Unfortunately, no school would take her. Her grades were too low, and other applicants were so much stronger.

Liza enjoyed spending money in college, and she bought great clothes. She saw her old friends every weekend, and she used her weekend time the way she wanted to. But she never became a psychologist.

Dean's commentary

In a sense, Liza's focus on fashion — always wanting "more" and "better" and "newer" — was her downfall. She worked too many hours to buy clothes. And because she worked all of those hours, she felt that she "really needed to play" when she wasn't working. Between waiting tables and playing, she squeezed out all time for study. School was the number-three priority in her lineup. She was busy making herself happy *now*. She didn't focus on what would make her happy in the future.

Liza thought that her father and I were out of touch with what she and her friends knew college was *really* about: having a good time and being independent. Unfortunately, Liza exercised her independence but not her good judgment. Adding up the hours she spent at school, work, and play should have told her that. Her study schedule was really out of balance. Liza's dad was essentially paying tuition so that Liza could wait tables and see her friends.

It's a hard reality of life: There's only so much time. You cannot create more of it, no matter what. THE major problem of students in academic trouble involves not controlling their time. It gets away from them, slipping away in hours, days, and weeks. The assignment that was weeks away is suddenly due this Friday!

To really use time — not waste it — you have to keep track of it, control it, *manage* it. You have to balance study, sports, social activities, clubs, and just "do-nothing" time. Schedule it all in — even the do-nothing time — or it won't get done. It's your life, not just a calendar. Make it work.

Can you do it?

Creating a **Personal Study Schedule** and following it are two very different things. Most students can make up pretty good schedules. Few students can follow them, at least not right away. *Making* a **Personal Study Schedule** requires attention to details and organization. *Following* your schedule requires discipline and determination to manage all that unscheduled time that college gives you. To be a successful student on your way to college, you have to make and follow your schedule now.

It's as simple as that to understand, but it is hard to do. Let the motivation of being an adult with a great job and career help you take scheduling your life NOW seriously.

Finally and most importantly, if you are a careless high school student whose courses are more of an aggravation than an opportunity, more of a nuisance than a challenge, you will never be a successful college student. Why? At the heart of scheduling is more than organization and control. Scheduling represents your sense of purpose as a college smart student. **RU READY?**

My Week in Review

	Sun	Mon	Tue	Wed	Thu	Fri	Sat
7:00							
8:00							
9:00							
10:00							
11:00							
12:00							
1:00							
2:00							
3:00							
4:00							
5:00							
6:00							
7:00							
8:00							
9:00							
10:00							
11:00	Go to Bed!	Go to Bed!	Go to Bed!	Go to Bed!	Go to Bed!		

A blank schedule for you. *Keep this copy clean so you can create enlarged photocopies of it.*

Personal Study Schedule

	Sun	Mon	Tue	Wed	Thu	Fri	Sat
7:00							
8:00							
9:00							
10:00							
11:00							
12:00							
1:00							
2:00							
3:00							
4:00							
5:00							
6:00							
7:00							
8:00							
9:00							
10:00							
11:00	Go to Bed!	Go to Bed!	Go to Bed!	Go to Bed!	Go to Bed!		

Personal Study Schedule (An Extra Copy For You!)

	Sun	Mon	Tue	Wed	Thu	Fri	Sat
7:00							
8:00							
9:00							
10:00							
11:00							
12:00							
1:00							
2:00							
3:00							
4:00							
5:00							
6:00							
7:00							
8:00							
9:00							
10:00							
11:00	Go to Bed!	Go to Bed!	Go to Bed!	Go to Bed!	Go to Bed!		

A blank schedule for you. *Keep this copy clean so you can create enlarged photocopies of it.* **RU READY?**

Cram, cram, cram...

I plan for tests. I feel great!

Strategy 9

All about tests —

test — noun. 1) a device for teachers to inflict pain on students;
2) the reverse is also true (not from Webster's Dictionary)

You know the drill. Multiple choice. True or False. Fill in the blank. Matching. You've seen them all. TESTS! And, unfortunately, tests aren't going to go away anytime soon. In fact, in one way or another, your life will be filled with tests, even after you've finished school, so you need to find a way to succeed with them. Some tests are just plain difficult for everyone. Other tests are personally challenging for you. Whatever the case, succeeding with tests takes planning and stamina. Read on to find out what that means.

Learn about yourself

On a scale of 1 (lowest) to 5 (highest), rate yourself on these test-preparation strategies.

_____ Preparing for tests without cramming.

_____ Keeping a file of the tests you've taken for each course. If the teacher has collected them, ask if you can keep a copy.

_____ Reviewing graded tests carefully to understand your mistakes — and reviewing the tests with teachers, if necessary.

_____ Anticipating what questions will be on the next test.

_____ Seeing your teacher or guidance counselor when you get several disappointing test grades.

_____ Scheduling more study time after low test grades.

_____ Talking to your teacher before "hard" tests.

_____ Recording test dates on your calendar so they never can sneak up on you.

Be college smart. Remember what we said earlier about school? Even when you don't like it, or parts of it, you must at least *respect it*. The same advice applies here. *Respect tests.* Why? Tests can move you ahead or stop you dead in your tracks. Tests are the name of the game. Learn to take and succeed with tests now.

Tests, tests, tests

Short ones, long ones. Easy ones, hard ones. Exams and quizzes. Take-homes, surprise tests. Oral tests. Some tests are standardized; some aren't. Fill in the circles or answer in brief paragraphs. The variety of tests is limited only by the variety of teachers and others who invent them.

How many tests have you had so far in your academic life? Hundreds? Thousands? How many more to come? Plenty. But the quantity is not as important as your attitude.

The student who goes into a test worrying about which questions he or she will get wrong probably is not well prepared for the test in the first place. This is a student who always studies for tests the same way: the day before, and in a hurry. This student is usually always behind in class. He or she never uses a Personal Study Schedule and never reads ahead of the course schedule. This student comes to class each day wondering what's going to happen. (This is the student who complains, *"I didn't know we were getting a test this week. Not another test!"*)

On the other hand, the student who takes a test and is eager to show what he or she knows is the student who is prepared. This student uses every class day to get ready for the next test or assignment. This student studies — doing more than the basic homework assignments. This student is college smart.

What tests really do

Why are you a student? To be educated? Yes. But very practically, because you eventually want to become "someone"— a stockbroker, or a lawyer, or a teacher, or an engineer, businessperson, scientist, doctor, etc. The path to these kinds of careers is long. And that path is filled with tests.

Many students don't see or understand the connection between (a) what they do in school each day, like taking tests, and (b) the demands of a career. One activity seems so distant from the other. Here's the connection. No matter what your future career or job, you will be tested every day by other people. In fact, that's what a job is: a position held by a person who has knowledge and skills and uses both to either answer questions or solve problems. Sounds a lot like a test, doesn't it? It is! Tests are a fact of life, part of every career. And you have to pass tests just to get to a career. You may as well start learning how to deal with tests if you want to succeed in life.

A future of answering questions

So one of the main purposes of education is to make you a good problem-solver or test-taker. Tests force you to gain knowledge, develop learning skills, and improve your powers of critical thinking. Put it another way: by taking tests, you are applying knowledge and using your intellectual skills to answer questions. It's a talent you'll use not only in college, but also later on in life. You'll constantly be asked questions. *How can I get this done? We have a problem — can you solve it? What do I do if ...? Do you know how to...?* In a job, people (bosses, customers, coworkers, clients, patients, etc.) are constantly testing your knowledge and your problem-solving skills.

While real life may *seem* to offer you more exciting kinds of tests than those in school, being tested as a person in a real job is still very much like being tested every day as a student. The main difference is this: When students get a low grade on a test, they can bring up their grade on the next test. Getting a low grade in a life situation is much more serious. Your auto mechanic's error could result in a serious accident. Your stockbroker's bad decision can cost you thousands of dollars. Your surgeon's poor judgment can cost you your life. Wrong answers in real life can result in any number of personal losses, discomforts, pain, and even tragedies.

Consider this for a moment: Computers are wonderful inventions that can help you in many ways. When you make a mistake on a computer, you hit the "undo" key. Unfortunately, in life, there are no "undo" keys. You have to live with the consequences of your mistakes. They are your responsibility. If you understand how tests in school prepare you for tests in life, you're on your way to avoiding many problems. It's a step you can be proud of. You are responsible for your successes, too!

How to think about tests

If you ask an athlete what he or she likes the most about a sport, one answer — if not THE answer — would be PLAYING IT. Not the practicing, the exercises, the wind sprints, or the weight-lifting. It's getting out on the field and trying your skill against an opponent. Competition and contests stir the blood. The challenge is to get it right, to win.

If you asked people who are musicians or actors why they enjoy what they do, their answer would probably be like the athlete's. They would tell you that practice can be tedious and tiring — but that the performance and the audience's applause make all the work worth it.

Is an athlete, musician, or actor really happy without competing and performing? Probably not. On the other hand, would most students be happy if school did not include tests? *YES! School would be great without tests!*

Even though tests are very much like competitions or performances, somehow, academic "contests" (tests) are not nearly as appealing. Why?

Face it. Many tests are boring and repetitive. And when tests are monotonous, they're unexciting. When they're unexciting, your interest fizzles, often along with your study time. More of the same old multiple-choice, fill-in-the-blank, compare/contrast, and matching stuff means you're more or less stuck with the same types of tests your grandparents took.

Just as you may have to bring interest to learning various subjects, you might have to bring — even create for yourself — an interest in tests. For students who have always "liked school," that's no problem. But others have to make an effort. Think of tests as important preparations for jobs and careers. This kind of thinking makes the effort worth it. Before you know it, you'll actually look forward to tests. You'll understand their practical purpose in your future: to eventually become an expert in some field — an expert who answers questions, solves problems, and understands complicated situations.

But what about right now? Want advantages for right now? How about the recognition of those around you? If someone asked you to name the "smart" kids in your class, you could do it. They take part in class discussion. They get high grades on tests. They seem always to be on top of their days. When you are one of the smart kids, others will recognize it, too. You'll have a reputation as someone who "has it together."

The same thing will happen in your future. Your reputation in your workplace will make you stand out as being an employee who can get the job done. You'll be marked as one of the people who is going places. Why? Because you can answer questions and solve difficult problems. Where will you develop those skills? In school.

You can't avoid tests, and excuses don't work.

I can't tell you the number of students who have sat across my desk and told me, *"I hate multiple-choice tests — they're tricky."* Or, *"I don't like essay tests. I can't think on my feet."* Plus, many students try to excuse their falling grades by saying, *"I like this kind of test, but not that kind."* *"I do well in this kind of test, but not that kind."*

You have to learn to become a universal test-taker. Think about the next BIG TESTS in your life: the ACT and the SAT. The competition to get into college is too tough for you to say to a college admissions counselor, *"I've got really high grades, but I just don't do well on standardized tests, and so my scores don't really reflect my ability."* Will that explanation work? Will it get you into your favorite college? No. The counselor will simply accept another student with your same grade point average who did well on the ACT or SAT.

After college, what happens when you decide you want to go to law school? You'll be up against the LSAT (the equivalent of the ACT for law school admission). And even though you write brilliant essays and have an excellent grade point average, if you can't get a high enough score on the LSAT, a law school won't accept you. Then, if you *do* get into a law school, what happens when you graduate? You'll have to face the state bar exam before you're allowed to practice law.

Almost all education after college requires that you prove your aptitude on a standardized test before you enter a program: You take the GMAT to enter business schools for an MBA, you take a GRE to enter graduate school, you take an MCAT to be a doctor, and so on and on and on. You may ask, *"Do the tests ever end?"* No.

Therefore, if you are not good at taking standardized tests, you have to LEARN how to handle them. Practice with software, or rehearse with test-preparation books. You can even take courses from private test-prep services. Start taking the ACT or SAT early and often. Pay the small fee that the testing service charges to send you the answer key with your scores. Then analyze where and why you make mistakes.

Some people just have a knack for taking standardized tests — they are really good at it. Other students have to learn to take tests, just like they learn anything else. If you're one of those students, you may have to work at it. Saying *"I'm not good with tests"* is no longer an excuse for a poor performance. It simply won't cut it.

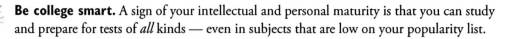 **Be college smart.** A sign of your intellectual and personal maturity is that you can study and prepare for tests of *all* kinds — even in subjects that are low on your popularity list.

As this Strategy tells you, you can't get away from tests. They will follow you through life, either as entrance exams or certifying tests for a profession. Plus, even if you don't intend to continue your education after college, you'll find yourself in situations in which your boss, your customers, or your clients are "testing" your competence. You have to be able to do well in these situations.

Some compass points on test-taking

You have probably read lots of tips about preparing for and taking tests. You know, getting enough sleep, reading questions carefully, checking your answers, etc. The tips are usually very good, and, like warming-up exercises, they can help you avoid "mental cramping." Here are some more ideas about tests. Some may be familiar — some may be new to you. All are important.

Before the test

Talk to your teacher several days before the test. Don't wait until the last minute. If you are unsure of some course material, go to the teacher *before the test* for help. It's just silly to hope that the troublesome material won't appear on the test.

Study everything, even though you know that everything can't be on the test. No test covers everything. But you should study everything, just in case a certain fact, term, or formula appears on the test. Knowing everything and developing test-preparation skills help you later on in college. Remember: In high school, you're building a knowledge/learning base for college. Make it a strong one. Strong test-taking skills are a big building block for that base.

Practice, practice, practice. Just as you practice free throws for basketball or learn your lines for a play, you prepare for tests every day, learning as you go: by keeping up with (or ahead of) the class, doing homework carefully, and studying with concentration. Develop a routine. Do extra math problems, reread your class notes or chapter, outline important information, create charts and flash cards that you can easily pick up and study — again and again, even while waiting for the bus! All these activities help you memorize things like foreign-language vocabulary, biology terms, names, events, and dates in history.

Review your Study Brief. What's a Study Brief? It's all of the important information for the test that you've collected and written out on one or two sheets of paper so you can view highlights at a glance. Just *making* this sheet is a form of studying and preparing for the test. As you wait for the test to be passed out, give your Study Brief one more look, a last-minute review of the critical information.

Don't procrastinate. Has this ever happened to you? You've got a few days before a test, and a little voice in the back of your head starts talking, saying, *"I know that I'm not very prepared to take Thursday's test, but I think I know enough. I'll risk it. I can hold off and just study Wednesday night. It'll be okay."*

This is typical procrastinator talk. Students who put off daily study already know that there are gaping holes in their knowledge. For them, closely looking at the material too soon before the test is scary. It tells them just HOW MUCH they don't know. It would be a lot of work to catch up. They don't want to face it, so they choose to wait until the last minute to cram and hope for the best.

Don't cram. Most students review seriously right before any test, especially big tests — that's natural. But there's a big difference between "a reviewer" and "a crammer." For the crammer, this last-minute preparation is the only serious studying he or she has done for the test. If there weren't tests, these students probably wouldn't study at all! They skim along the surface of their courses from day to day, just getting the big concepts mentioned in class.

They wait until one or two nights before the test. Then they really plunge into course material to cram, running at full speed. They may even pull an all-nighter.

The crammer hopes the information will stay in his or her brain just long enough to get through the test. Some students get really good at cramming — they even get pretty good grades on tests they've crammed for.

But if you think back to the introduction to this book, you'll recall the real tragedy of cramming: The knowledge gained is temporary. It's called short-term learning, and it means your mind holds information for a brief time, and then the information's gone for good, as if your mind never held it in the first place. Crammers never become college smart.

Crammers finish courses, semesters, and even four years of high school with little or no knowledge. Because crammers forget most of what they crammed, when they get to college, these students don't have the knowledge to keep up with college courses. Cramming is one of the major reasons that huge numbers of students drop out or take extra years to finish college. But that won't happen to you if you're a college smart student.

During the test

No gimmicks can replace being well-prepared for a test. But here are some strategies to help you make the best use of your test-taking time under stressful conditions.

Read test questions CAREFULLY. The number-one rule when taking any test is to read the questions carefully. In fact, read every question at least twice before you answer it. There is nothing worse than getting a test back and seeing that you lost points on a question when you knew the right answer! You just didn't understand what the question was asking, and so your answer was wrong.

Always read the test from beginning to end before you answer any questions. Some students are afraid to discover the hard questions that come later in the test. To do your best, you have to know what you're dealing with from the outset.

Most of the time, you don't have to answer questions in any particular order. Use this freedom to your advantage. You can answer the questions in any order that is comfortable for you. Do the easy questions first (to score "sure points" right away) or the hard ones first (to get them off your mind). Do what works best for you.

Gather your thoughts. Close your eyes for a few seconds before you start to answer. Use this time to relax your mind and relax your breathing.

Wear a watch or sit where you can see a clock. Don't lose track of time. If you do, you won't get to all the questions.

Look at the sections of the test. If you can, estimate how long each section will take to complete. Now watch the clock, so you can pace yourself and complete all the test questions.

Don't understand a question? Raise your hand and ask the teacher to rephrase it or ask, *"Do you mean ....?"*

Essay/paragraph answers? Jot down key points before starting to write. Use these key points as your outline. Otherwise, you run the risk of rambling off the main points and never returning to them.

Don't leave any essay question unanswered. Even if you don't think you know the answer, write whatever you know that relates to the question.

Take care of personal needs. Make sure you go to the bathroom before a test. Dress comfortably. Get tissues or cough drops if you have a cold. Do what you can to eliminate personal distractions.

Crunched for time? Work on the questions with higher point values.

Check for careless mistakes. If time permits, go over your answers to catch errors caused by stress.

Stay focused. Don't let small annoyances distract you: the siren on the street outside, the kid who taps his pencil or blows his nose. If the door down the hall bangs, don't look up. None of it is important at the moment. Shut it all out and concentrate on the test.

When you get the test back

Wrong answers are just as important as right answers. When you get a test back, don't just look at the grade and then throw the test in your backpack or in the trash can. Look at those wrong answers. Ask yourself, *"Did I get them wrong because I didn't know the answer, or because I made a careless error?"*

- *If your grade is the result of not knowing the subject well enough.* There are two obvious remedies. (1) Put in more *time* studying and (2) see your teacher (or your guidance counselor) about your study habits. Maybe you need to change your study schedule. Perhaps you're missing a better or smarter way to tackle this subject.

- *If you have a pattern of careless errors.* Recognize it, and be more careful next time. (Getting enough sleep? Not reading directions carefully? Not looking at the entire test before you start so you can pace yourself?)

If you don't understand why you got an answer wrong, go over your test with the teacher. *And don't go to the teacher just to try to scavenge extra points by arguing.* You need to figure out what you misunderstood, so you don't make the same mistakes on the next test.

Tests: Who's responsible?

Understand this: **Disappointing test grades are your fault.** Not the fault of the teacher. Not the fault of the subject, which you might not like. And not the fault of the tests you are taking. *The worst thing a serious test-taker can do is make excuses or assign blame to others.* You must learn to take tests, just as you learn algebra, foreign language, or composition. There are a lot of poor test-takers out there because they don't accept test-taking as a skill that requires development. Don't be one of them.

Grade Grubbing (Digging for something that just ain't there)

Have you heard the term *grade grubbing?* While you might not have heard the term, grade grubbing exists. Grubbers are students who receive a graded test or assignment and then dig around to see if they can find little complaints to bring to the teacher in the hope of gaining a point here or there. When these kinds of students start to approach a teacher, the teacher's reaction is to hide under a desk, or run off to the dentist — even without an appointment.

It's one thing to find a legitimate grading error on your test. If the teacher agrees it is an error, then the teacher will change your grade. The teacher may even decide that something is wrong with the test question. If so, he or she will raise the grades of *all* students in the class who lost points on that item. It's quite another thing for a student to grub only for him or herself. This student is playing a game, often trying to repair the damage of a too-low grade *after* the test, rather than studying carefully *before* it. Don't become a member of the Grub Club. Already a member? Don't renew your membership.

Grubbers are closely related to students who view themselves as victims. They always find excuses for low test grades, blaming the teacher: *"The teacher doesn't like me"* or *"I can never understand what the teacher is saying."* If these students don't understand what's being said in class, they had better see the teacher to talk about the problem.

ACTs and SATs — This is the big time!

When you were in grade school, you took standardized tests, but no one ever told you to prepare for them. You knew they were coming sometime. But you just showed up one day at school and your teacher handed you a test and a sharp pencil.

Now that you are older, things are very different. College admissions tests — SATs and ACTs — are in a separate category because these are your first *qualifying* tests. Your scores on these tests either open or close doors to your future. You need to prepare seriously for them. But here's the good news: by preparing for them, you will improve your scores.

ACTs and SATs are mostly multiple-choice tests, although the SAT includes an essay (required) and the ACT offers one (optional). Some colleges require an ACT essay. Others do not. The ACT and SAT will stretch your thinking skills and test your knowledge as never before! The questions are more complex, so the tests require more preparation.

As much as you've developed test-taking skills in your courses, you'll need to develop some new skills just for standardized tests. Visit the SAT and ACT Web sites; they give very good introductions to these tests. Log on and learn about them. Also get some "prep" books or software and practice. Then go talk to your guidance counselor about how to take these tests.

Know this: Standardized tests are here to stay; you can't escape them. You will have to take the SAT or ACT — or both — to qualify for college. Later in your education, you may also have to take one of these "alphabet" tests, too: GRE, LSAT, MCAT, DAT, and GMAT. While standardized tests evaluate only a part of your intellect — and nothing about your maturity or motivation — they are still challenges you must confront and learn to manage. Develop your skills for taking standardized tests NOW so they don't become an obstacle to entering college or to other opportunities in your future.

Listen to Dr. Bob —

Why you need to practice this Strategy for college

As this Strategy said, you will be tested your entire life. However, in college, the pressure is more intense than in high school. Unlike high school teachers, who may give dozens of quizzes and tests in an 18-week course, some college instructors may give only a midterm and a final exam. When you have only two or three tests per course, your performance on each one is critical. Some students like to wait to see what they get on the first test before they decide how much they have to study for a course. That's just not smart. You can't afford to take that risk. In college, if you mess up on the first test out of three, you're in trouble.

Here's another reason that test performance is critical. Your test grades in college can't be improved by that old high school remedy: doing extra credit. Some high school students have gotten into the habit of asking for extra credit projects to offset not-so-good test grades. Don't get into that habit. Extra credit hardly ever exists in college — your test grades stand on their own.

Whenever you feel down and wonder why you have to be doing all this "learning stuff," recall that your life *after* graduation requires the same skills you need *in* school. So even if you don't always like the daily school routine, maintain your respect for it. Because when the curtain goes up the opening night of your life after college graduation, you want to know your part really well — well enough to get the applause you deserve in the form of success and rewards.

PSST! Look at your answers in this Strategy's **Learn about yourself.** The items are really a list of ways to prepare for tests. How does your approach to taking tests stack up to tips in the list? Then go back over the highlighted passages in this Strategy. How much of this info did you already know?

Congratulate yourself on everything you're doing right! Do you have habits to change?

Go back through the Strategy and put a check mark in the margin next to each point you have to work on. As the school year progresses, return to your checked sections frequently to see how well you are improving. Don't let tests be obstacles to your success! It's a lesson you can learn from the next **Up close and personal.**

<u>Up close and personal</u>

Jason: Wishing doesn't make it happen.

Jason wanted to go to just one university all his life. His father had graduated from this university, and so had Jason's older brother. Jason followed the university's football team fanatically. Since he was a small boy, his bedroom had been filled with the university's banners and posters. His dad bought season tickets, and Jason never missed a game.

This university was the place for Jason, and as far as he was concerned, he was already in — even before he had filled out an application. Jason saw me early in his junior year of high school. I told him that he really had to prepare for his standardized tests. Jason's PLAN and PSAT scores (tests taken in the early years of high school) were already predicting that his ACT and SAT scores would not make him stand out in a crowd of college applicants. He had to do better. He had to study before he took the tests. It was his responsibility.

He took both the ACT and SAT twice, preparing for them very little, and his scores were pretty borderline.

When it became time to apply for admission, I advised Jason that because his test scores and his grades (a **B+** average) were good but not great, he needed an edge. His best bet was to get his application in as early as possible. Even with that advice, he waited longer than should have. For three years, the university had been flooded with applicants and had cut off applications early. That story was all over the local evening news and in the newspapers. Jason knew about it.

With so many students applying to the university, the competition was going to be very tough, and Jason's test scores were going to hurt him — even with an early application.

In November, Jason received a letter from the university: *"We regret to inform that given the large numbers of applicants, we cannot offer you admission."* Stunned, Jason called the university's Admissions Office and asked why he wasn't accepted. Their answer: Jason's test scores did not fall within the acceptable range. *"But,"* argued Jason, *"my grade point average is **B+**, and I took part in lots of extracurricular activities in high school."*

The counselor simply repeated that Jason's test scores were too low. She invited Jason to take the test again and apply again next year. She was sorry, but Jason was no longer eligible to apply for this year.

Now that it was too late, Jason was suddenly prepared to do anything to get into this university. He asked about going to another school freshman year and then transferring. Could he do that? What grades would he need to be able to transfer? What courses should he take?

Jason missed his opportunity. Why? He didn't take standardized tests seriously. Like many students, Jason thought that "good" grades and extracurricular activities would offset "average" test scores. In fact, a **B+** grade point average is average these days for college applicants, so it confirmed how "average" Jason was. The students he was competing against for admission were offering much higher ACT and SAT scores. Why would the university admit him when it could admit much better students?

Dean's commentary

Too many students think of ACT and SAT tests as though they were vision tests. You just go in and read the chart. It will tell you the condition of your eyes. True, you can't prepare for a vision test. Your vision is what it is.

Not so with standardized tests. These aren't IQ tests. The ACT tests you on academic subjects, and the SAT tests math and verbal abilities as well as your natural intelligence. These tests want to know *what you have learned* throughout your education. That's a big difference from taking a vision test. *It means that you CAN study for these tests.* The more you practice, the higher your scores. If you want higher scores, prepare for them. Your success is your responsibility.

Here are your options. Some high schools run help sessions for preparing for the ACT and SAT. Bookstores are full of prep books with sample problems to acquaint you with the kinds of questions you'll face. There are software programs so you can practice on your computer. There are test-prep services — and even local colleges — that will conduct courses to help you succeed with these tests.

Jason had gone to the meetings that his high school conducted for seniors applying to college. He even came to see me for more information. For the most part, he listened, but he ignored the part about making sure his grades and test scores were good enough for the college he was applying to. Jason didn't "get" it.

- First, he didn't research the scores that the university required for admission.

- Second, he didn't understand the need to prepare for standardized tests as you would prepare for an athletic competition — you train and practice.

- Third, he ignored my advice to apply to more than one college. Like many students, he thought that applying to only one college, and saying with enthusiasm that it was his favorite, would get him in.

Jason may have known the win-loss record of his favorite university's football team, the stats for each player, and the fine points of the coach's strategy against various opponents. However, he didn't give enough attention to other facts about the school: the qualifications for admission. For three years, the university had been swamped with applications. That's the way it's going to be for most schools for the next few years because of the bulge in the college-age population. Competition, therefore, will be tough.

Jason, like so many students, never believed that he would be denied his dream. He was not accepted by his favorite university. As it turns out, the plays in his college strategy book were all wrong. **RU READY?**

Tracking my grades helps keep me on top!

Strategy 10
Tracking grades —
getting from here to there takes more than hope and luck

Here's another major strategy for controlling your courses. As you move through a semester, do you ever pause to gauge how well you are doing in each of your courses? Or do you just "wait and see" what your final grade will be? That's a little like whitewater kayaking without a paddle: You're letting the rapids sweep you along. You should be controlling the kayak so that you don't hit the rocks or capsize! This Strategy will give you the paddle and the navigational know-how to get yourself safely through each semester's waters.

Learn about yourself

Mark the statement that best describes you.

How do you think about grades during the semester?

_____ I don't think about grades. I just take each test and assignment as they come. Whatever they add up to will be my final grade.

_____ I let teachers keep track of my grades. Isn't that what they're supposed to do?

_____ I have a vague idea of my grades because I try to remember them, but there are so many. Sometimes grades on report cards surprise me because I thought I was doing better than I actually was.

_____ I worry about grades a lot. So I really hope for the best.

_____ I know the last grade I got on a test, but I don't do such a good job of remembering the grades on tests before that.

_____ I keep a record of all my grades in my course notebooks.

The importance of scoreboards

While sitting at a high school basketball game, I noticed that I was constantly looking up at the scoreboard. After every basket, I would look up to check the score: back and forth from the action on the court to the scoreboard. Finally, I asked myself *why?* The score was changing by only two or three points. Why wasn't I just keeping the score in my head and concentrating on the game?

My answer was that checking the scoreboard so often was part of my enjoyment of the game (so long as my team was winning, of course). I wanted to see that my team was really four points ahead, eight points ahead — or sometimes coming up from behind and needing only six points to tie. Seeing that score change was almost as important as watching the ball go through the home team's hoop.

Each semester is like watching several games (courses) with a lot of points (grades). As with scoreboard watching, you should pay attention to all your grades on tests, quizzes, and assignments. True, when grades in a certain course are not very good or dipping, looking at a *B-* or *C* (or worse) isn't much fun. But checking your "score" each time you get a grade is very important. It's how you stay involved in all your courses. It's a way of being in control. If your grades are generally high, you're winning — you're doing the right things in managing your courses. If your grades dip, you need to change something. The low test score is telling you something's wrong, and you have to change your "game strategy."

What you need, then, is a "scoreboard" for each of your courses. And each scoreboard should list all your grades for that course as the semester moves along. That's how you keep track of your progress. That's how you know if your study efforts are paying off.

Academic scoreboards

Your academic scoreboard is a grade diary that you create in each of your course notebooks. Remember: we agreed you should have a notebook for every course. That notebook is the place where you keep all your course information: things like course outlines, notes, assignment sheets, and study summaries. Your grade diary, let's call it a **Grade Tracker**, is one of those important items. You can use a single page in your notebook to track your grades, or you can keep a separate sheet in the pocket of each notebook. (Just don't lose that sheet of paper!)

Making a **Grade Tracker** for each course is one of the things you should do during the first two weeks of the semester. Your **Grade Tracker**, your academic scoreboard, should have five columns. You'll find a sample at the end of this Strategy that you can photocopy if you don't want to make your own. You can also download a **Tracker** from **www.areyoureallyreadyforcollege.com**. Here's how a **Grade Tracker** looks.

Quizzes, tests, labs, assignments, etc.	Grade earned	%age of final grade	%age of grade earned so far	Current average

- The first column lists the item graded. Was it a test, a quiz, a lab, a paper, another kind of graded assignment? Record the item in this column.

- In the second column, you write in the grade you earned.

- In the third column, you record how much each grade counts. In other words, what percentage does this grade contribute to your final grade? For example, 5%, 10%? 15%, 20%? 25%? Often you'll find this information in your course outline. Or your teacher will tell you in class how his or her grading system works.

- The fourth column shows how much of your final grade you've earned so far in a course. Have your earned 15% of your final grade? 50% of your final grade? Think of it this way: If your courses suddenly "stopped," this would be the grade you earned.

- The fifth column shows your current grade. We'll talk more about this column in a moment.

To show you how the **Grade Tracker** works, let's use an example. On the first day of the semester, your history teacher, like all your teachers, hands out a course outline (a syllabus). You've read it carefully. One of the many things it explains about the course is how your teacher will calculate your final grade.

Let's say the course outline tells you that you will have 5 tests, 10 quizzes, and 2 papers to write, and as always, there will be a final exam.

- Each quiz is worth 2% of your final grade.

  10 quizzes = 20% of your grade.

- Each test is worth 10% of your final grade.

  5 tests = 50% of your grade.

- Each paper is worth 5% of your final grade.

  2 papers = 10% of your grade.

- Your final examination = 20% of your final grade.

  20% (quizzes)
  50% (tests)
  10% (papers)
  <u>20% (final exam)</u>
  100%

Now imagine that you've begun the semester and after a few weeks, this is how you do:

You take a quiz and get an 85%.

You take a test and get a 90%.

You write a paper and get a 95%.

So after completing these three parts of your history course, you have earned 17% of your final grade. Here's how your **Grade Tracker** should look.

Quizzes, tests, labs, assignments, etc.	Grade earned	%age of final grade	%age of grade earned so far	Current average
Quiz #1	85%	2%	2%	
Test #1	90%	10%	12%	
Paper #1	95%	5%	17%	

Be college smart. Just keeping this simple chart will help you see where you are "grade-wise" in each of your courses. That's important. Tracking your grades will help you avoid that kind of grade "daze" that students get when they must keep track of so many grades in several courses. In such a daze, students lose track of the large picture: *that, with every grade, they are slowly developing a final grade.*

The value of knowing the score

If your grades on tests and assignments are always *A*s, that's great. You know where you stand. But you still want to keep your chart up to date just to see how far along you are in each course. Have you earned 30% of your final grade? 50% of your final grade? Or do you have an *A* after completing 70% of the coursework? With 70% of your work behind you, that *A* is looking more and more solid.

But if your grades vary or are slipping, you need to know right away. Have you ever heard anyone say that *knowledge is power?* Knowing your grade after each quiz, test, or paper gives you power. The minute you understand that something is wrong, you can take steps to correct the problem. You can find a way to correct the problem by examining study habits or test-taking skills. You can do things *to control the course.*

Filling in the 5th column

So in our history-course example, with nearly 20% of your grade behind you, what's your score (your final grade so far)? You have the information to fill in the first four columns with numbers, but what about the fifth? You can't just add up these numbers and divide by 3, because these items all have different "weights"— that is, some grades count more than others. In our example, the quiz grade is only 2% of your grade, while the test counts 10%.

That's what makes the 5th column difficult to fill in. Some teachers use a point system, some use percentages, and some grade on a curve. Doing the math can become confusing. Fortunately, your school probably sends out quarterly grades so that you know where you stand in each course when you receive this grade report. But to be in control of your grades, you don't want to wait for the next report. You'll want to know right away, right after that last hard test or after that long paper. Your solution? Remember **Strategy 5: Talking to teachers**. They can do the math for you.

Early in the semester, explain to each teacher that you're the kind of student who likes to keep close track of your course progress. Ask if it's okay for you to check in often to see where you stand grade-wise. Most teachers will be happy to help you. When you go to check on your current grade, you can also ask any questions you may have. For example, the grade on your paper may be very good but your quiz grades are falling. Why is that? You and the teacher can talk about it. Or the teacher may tell you what made your paper so good. You can use that information to make papers in all of your classes better. Checking your grades with your teachers gives you a way to talk about your work and gives your teachers the opportunity to advise and help you.

Be sure you understand clearly why you're tracking grades: It is a way of closely monitoring your progress in your courses. But also be academically mature, and remember that LEARNING is the real goal. If you're getting good grades by cramming, you'll pay for it later. Don't be the kind of student who worries only about grades.

Using what you know

Let's switch classes for a moment and look at your **Tracker** in chemistry.

Quizzes, tests, labs, assignments, etc.	Grade earned	%age of final grade	%age of grade earned so far	Current average
Quiz #1	89%	5%	5%	89
Lab #1	93%	5%	10%	91
Quiz #2	90%	5%	15%	89
Test #1	85%	20%	35%	87

You know that with 35% of your grade in, you have a **B** in the course. What else do you know? You did better on your lab assignment than the test. Another thing you now know is that you didn't study enough for the test. Next question: What are you going to do about it? You'd better do something. Why? Most courses build on earlier information. If you don't "get" the early information, it will continue to hurt you. Plus, courses typically get harder as the semester moves on. Later, you'll struggle even more. In other words, you've got mostly **B**s on the *easy* part of the semester. If you don't increase your study hours and/or improve your study strategy for the rest of the semester, your grades are very likely to continue to fall — or you'll stay stuck at the **B** level. I'll tell you more about the problem of **B**s in a minute.

Ask yourself this: Did your grade fall on Test #1 because of short-term learning? Might be. Here's what I mean. You got two slightly better grades on small units of information (two quizzes), but when you got to the larger test, *essentially a review of the material so far,* your grade wasn't as good. Hmmm….

In this example, grade tracking tells you that your chemistry course needs an extra push — 35% of your grade is currently less than an **A**. And the course will only get harder. You need to do some serious talking — with your teacher and with your counselor.

What you DON'T say is *"I'm just not that good in chemistry."* You could be "good" if you improved your study strategies.

What you DON'T say is *"Well I can bring my grade up later."* That's a good idea, but how are you going to do it, and *when* are you going to get started? *Later* can be a dangerous word to students.

What you DON'T say is *"That **B** is not so bad."* You might not still have that **B** as the material gets harder, and a **B** is bad. Why do you need an **A**? Why isn't a **B** good enough? Are you college-bound? Read on.

Some fine points of grade tracking — pluses and minuses

You need to know that, generally speaking, today's high schools give higher grades to students than schools did in the past. As a student who will be applying to college, you should know that almost half of all college-bound students graduate with *A* averages. College admissions offices are used to seeing *A*s on student records. Therefore, the difference between an *A* and an *A+* becomes significant to these reviewers. Quite frankly, *B*s aren't very impressive in the world of pre-college grades these days.

When so many college-bound students have *A*s, college admissions offices must make distinctions, so pluses and minuses on grades become more significant than ever. *B* grades (or lower) stick out like sore thumbs. This makes grade-tracking even more important. When a test grade lowers your grade average, even in the middle of a course, that's a big deal. You better start controlling the course and asking yourself what you need to do to turn this around. How? Read on.

When your grades slide

When your **Grade Tracker** signals that it's time to make an appointment with a teacher or counselor, your goal during the appointment is to get advice about changing your study strategies. More study time is usually the answer. As we've said many times, learning takes time. However, often, it's the way you are attacking the subject that's holding you back. Either way, talking regularly with your teachers and guidance counselor will make a difference.

Also, investigate what's going on in your days. Maybe your study place needs some "renovation." Are you getting enough sleep? What if the course giving you trouble is the first class of your day, and you've gotten into the habit of watching late-night shows on TV? (Record them and watch them some other time.)

The important thing is this: When you are a student, you are a student all day long. Yes, you do other things, but they are in addition to your student responsibilities. Being a student is central to your life, and other things have to find a place around your school commitments. So if being an athlete or working a part-time job means you can't fit in enough study time — or makes you too tired when you try to study — you must adjust these things so they no longer interfere with your student life.

True, your final grades will clearly tell you how well you controlled and used your time to study for your courses. But if you wait until the end of each semester to evaluate your efforts, you can end up with a set of final grades that will really tarnish your overall record. *Grade Trackers identify a problem while there's still time to fix it.*

Understand this: One semester's low grades damage your overall grade point average. Here's how it works. Let's say that after an unsuccessful semester, the next semester, you work really hard to try to bring up your overall grade point average. Your efforts pay off. But after all that effort, earning *really high grades* second semester only returns you to the average you had before your grades fell. In such circumstances, you've eaten up a whole year, first damaging your grade point average and then trying to recover it. And we're not even talking about all the knowledge you lost in the first semester.

Stay off the academic roller coaster, which takes you up sometimes and drops you down at others. You're far better off if you control your life, applying the sound Strategies of this guidebook and working steadily each semester to maintain your grades.

Grade-tracking and getting into college

As a student planning on college, you will apply to college when you *start* your senior year. That means that college admission counselors will be evaluating just three years of your high school work. What if you didn't really "get going" until the middle of your sophomore year? That means only half of your high school record will impress the admissions counselor. Start grade tracking as soon as you start high school, or as soon as you can. Remember the high number of *A*s other students are earning. You must have them, too, to compete.

Tracking puts you in control.

So from the first week of the semester, make sure you know how your final grade is going to be calculated in every course. As I said earlier, most teachers spell things out in the course outline (syllabus) handed out at the start of the semester. By reading this outline, you can see how many assessments you will have in a course and how much each counts toward your final grade. If a teacher does not explain to the class how grades are calculated at the start of the term, find out in your conversation with the teacher during **The first two weeks** (Strategy 3).

Some teachers may "wing it," giving as many assignments and tests as they feel are "needed" as the semester moves along. However, even they can give you a good idea of how your final grade will be determined.

Why do you need this information? To be in control. To control a course, you must have a sense of the importance of all its graded parts: assignments, projects, labs, tests, quizzes, speeches, etc. If you know this from the start, you can then see the BIG PICTURE in each course. You'll know how each bit of work you do either adds to or subtracts from your grade.

Once you know how the teacher will calculate your final grade, you can evaluate your effort. And that gives you *more power.* This power will prevent you from making mistakes. For example, you won't kid yourself into thinking that your good grade on a quiz that counts 10% of your grade will offset that poor test grade worth 25%.

> **Be college smart.** Knowing how your final grade is calculated puts you in control. It also shows you clearly where you stand by pointing out the weights of each of your grades as the semester progresses.

What's more, knowing the teacher's grading system means you can plan your semester around it. *Got a cross-country event coming up right before a test that counts a lot?* You can't afford to do poorly on such an important test. *How can you adjust your schedule to make time for a good review?* PLAN AHEAD.

Keep your **Grade Tracker** in your course notebook — and use it. Review it often. Pay attention to what it's telling you on a grade-by-grade basis. Your tracker gives you important information about your study efforts. Here's how:

- *If studying isn't paying off,* you have to adjust something — either the amount of time you're putting into the course or the way you are studying. Talk to your teacher or guidance counselor if you can't figure out what's wrong. For example, let's say that your last two grades in foreign language have dropped. Your teacher may tell you that you are just memorizing vocabulary but forgetting rules of grammar. Now you know how to focus your study to better your grade. Your **Grade Tracker** prompted the talk with your teacher, which, in turn, gave you information you needed to do better on future tests.

- *If studying is paying off,* the grades you record in your **Tracker** will confirm that what you are doing to study for each course is working. You probably don't need to adjust anything. Just remember what is working so well for you, so you can apply it to other courses in the future. Don't get overconfident and slack off on your efforts. They're working! Keep going.

In either case, the tracker has given you the information that you can use. You'll be in control. This is the kind of independence that keeps you making headway!

To recap: 5 ways tracking controls your courses.

1. You'll know how many assessments you have in a course and how much each counts toward your final grade.

2. You'll know how each bit of work you do either adds to or subtracts from your grade.

3. Knowing the teacher's grading system means you can plan your semester activities around preparing for graded events, like tests, projects, and papers.

4. Your **Grade Tracker** evaluates your study efforts, telling you whether or not you are studying enough.

5. Tracking puts you in control of the course and your grades. Remember that kayak we mentioned in the first paragraph of this Strategy? Tracking prevents you from being swept away by the strong currents — or smashed against the rocks.

So track your grades in all your courses and know how each counts toward your final grade. You'll be amazed how much this tracking helps you stay focused on your progress. Think of it as "keeping score." And when a family member asks you how you're doing in Chemistry, you might reply, "*Well, 40% of the course is completed* (in grade time) *and I've got an A-.*" Plus, you can say it with confidence. You could even say to yourself, "*I know what to do to bring it up to an A.*"

Listen to Dr. Bob —

Why you need to practice this Strategy for college

You can take the habit of grade-tracking to college, where it is more important than ever. Why? Because college courses frequently offer you fewer tests and other grading opportunities than you have in high school. A college course might have only two to three tests. Bomb the first test, and you may not recover.

Grade-tracking is one more way to control your grades. It confirms that you are managing your studies, doing the ongoing studying that learning requires. When you are learning, your grades won't disappoint you.

PSST! By now, you know the drill. Go back over the highlights. Read them now and reread them often. Why? This book of Strategies is a guidebook. It's not something that you read once and put away. In fact, think of it like a map that is giving you directions to a remote destination through territory you've never seen before. Always keep your guidebook close to you. The landscape you have to cover can be downright scary at times, so your map is essential. But if you have it with you every step of the way, I guarantee you will reach your destination. So review your map regularly. Sometimes you need to know where you have been to really appreciate where you are going.

<u>Up close and personal</u>

Kyle: He wasn't "watching his weight."

Most college courses have midterm exams so students can get a sense of how well they are doing in each course. Kyle came to see me three weeks after his midterms in the first semester of his sophomore year. He was a scholarship student and had to keep a certain grade point average to receive his scholarships. At midterms, Kyle had two *C*s, a *B*, and a *D* in his courses. He was in my office to talk about the *D* in history. At the bottom of the test, his instructor had written *"Think about dropping this course. See me."* Our conversation went something like this:

Dr. Bob: How have you done in history since the midterm test?

Kyle: Very much better. I got a *B*- on the last test. It's really coming together now.

Dr. Bob: That's great. Have you figured out what grades you need on the remaining tests and assignments to earn a high grade in the course? You'll need a high grade to keep your scholarships.

Kyle: Oh, I'll do fine. I've got two more tests and a paper to do yet.

Dr. Bob: But how do the two last tests and writing assignment contribute to your final grade?

Kyle: Blank stare.

Dr. Bob: What are they worth? How much do they count toward your final grade?

Kyle: (Pause) I don't know.

Dr. Bob: Isn't it on the course handout? You know, the course outline that you got at the beginning of the semester?

Kyle: Oh, yeah. I've got it in my folder somewhere. Wait. I'll look it up. (Digs through folder.) Here it is on the course outline. It says there are four tests and one writing assignment. The first three tests count 20% each, the paper is 10%, and the final exam is 30%.

Dr. Bob: Okay, let's do the math. What kind of *D* did you get on the midterm test? Did you just miss a *C*, or was it a low *D*?

Kyle: A low *D*. That's why the instructor thought I should maybe drop the course.

Dr. Bob: So you're saying that right now, with two of the four tests behind you, you've got about a *C-* in the course — the average of a *B-* and a *D*. And that's 40% of your grade, right?

Kyle: I guess, but I know I can bring the grade up. I'm getting it now.

Dr. Bob: You don't think you should drop the course?

Kyle: No, I dropped English last semester, and if I drop this, too, I'll be really far behind.

At the end of the semester, Kyle got a *B* in history, but it took so much effort that he let his other courses slip. He got three *C*s and a *D* in his other courses. He completely blew his final in math, which counted 40% of his grade, and he lost his scholarships.

Dean's commentary

What happened to Kyle? His first mistake: At the start of the semester, he didn't know how much each grade counted toward his final grade — in all his courses, not just history. Students who don't keep track of their grades lose sight of how they are really doing in a course. There are a couple of reasons this happens.

- Some students hope that if they keep improving, the instructor will grade them "on improvement," giving more weight to the grades at the end of the semester than the early ones. However, that rarely happens. Professors follow the grading policy stated in their course outlines.

- Other students prefer to stay unaware of their grades because it's too worrisome and stressful to think about them. They don't want to know how they are doing. They just keep hoping that something will happen that will work in their favor. When grades come out, these students may be shocked and disappointed by their grades, but there's nothing they can do about them.

Should Kyle have dropped the course when he realized he was in trouble? Probably, but even he recognized that he was developing a pattern of dropping courses. If you recall, he had already dropped a course during his last semester. Kyle had several problems going on here, and all of them contributed to losing his scholarship. He wasn't getting a jump-start on his courses, he wasn't keeping up, and then when he got behind and tried to repair the damage, there was too much work and not enough time. Keeping a **Grade Tracker** would have helped him see his predicament more clearly and make a better decision.

My Tracking Sheet   Course _____

Quizzes, tests, labs, assignments, etc.	Grade earned	%age of final grade	%age of grade earned so far	Current average

Log on to **www.areyoureallyreadyforcollege.com** *or* **www.rureallyready4college.com** *to download more tracking sheets.* **RU READY?**

Extracurricular activities and recommendations, too —
you need more than high grades

You choose people as friends because you like them personally and admire the things they do. When selecting students, colleges do the same thing. They want students who are personally outstanding, not just academically talented. These days, there are many more applicants than seats at good colleges, so admissions officers can afford to be choosey. In the next few years, the number of students headed for college will increase greatly. Extracurricular activities and letters of recommendation will become more and more important because both tell college admissions officers about the person inside the student. This information can make a big difference when selective colleges must choose certain students from among a large group of applicants — all with the same grades and test scores on their applications.

Learn about yourself _____

Check those that apply to you.

Note: extracurriculars are **all** non-classroom activities — in and out of school — that you do regularly.

When it comes to extracurricular activities, I —

_____ Generally ignore them.

_____ Do just a few and really devote quality time to each.

_____ Participate only in activities *away* from school (part-time jobs, scouting, clubs).

_____ Take part only in activities connected with school (sports, Key Club, drama club, etc.).

_____ Do only activities that I think will look good on a college application.

_____ Do what my friends do, so I can spend more time with them.

_____ Sign up for as many as I can.

List your extracurriculars and record the number of hours you spend on each per week.

Activity	Hours each week
1. _____	_____
2. _____	_____
3. _____	_____
4. _____	_____
5. _____	_____
6. _____	_____

Be college smart. More and more, the people who are going to decide if you are the kind of person they want in their colleges will be every bit as interested in your letters of recommendation and extracurricular record as your grades. The more competitive (hard to get into) the school, the more important extracurricular activities are for admissions. You should take them seriously.

About the nation's colleges

If you were to list all the nation's colleges, you'd have more than 2,000 schools, all with varying degrees of quality, and therefore with very different admissions standards.

The 300 or so colleges at the top of the list are very difficult to get into — and are getting more difficult to enter with every passing year. They have the highest admissions standards. They accept only those students with perfect grades from high schools with reputations for excellence. These students have completed challenging pre-college programs, scored exceptionally well on the ACT and/or SAT, and involved themselves in worthwhile activities outside the classroom. Letters of recommendation for these students will speak specifically about how the applicants will be valuable additions to a campus that is already filled with similarly qualified students. (We'll refer to these harder-to-get-into colleges as "competitive" or "selective" schools.)

The schools at the bottom of the list will take just about any student who applies for admission. Unfortunately, while you can easily be accepted by these schools, you won't get a very good education for your money.

The schools in the middle of the list will vary in their admissions qualifications. You can get a very good education at these colleges, but you have to take time to discover their qualities.

As you shop for colleges, you will want to choose a school that offers the programs you might be interested in. If you want to study to be a journalist, an engineer, a marine biologist, or a speech therapist, it only makes sense that the schools that catch your interest offer these programs. Then you must choose qualities in a college that suit you personally: for example, a large, middle, or small school; a school in or near a city, a small town, or someplace in between. After that, you must look at many more details about colleges to discover if they're right for you. Conversations with your teachers and counselors will really help you sort things out — just start early to think and talk about possible schools. You want to choose those that "fit" you.

But in the end, you want to get into the "best" college you can. Why? Because as you go up the list of colleges, the higher the school, the better the student body. You want to go to a school that has students like you: intelligent, hard-working, creative, interested in school, and friendly. The intellectual give-and-take among your fellow students will set the tone for your education, reinforcing its quality. When you finally graduate, you want to be able to say that your tuition dollars were well-spent.

Choosing the best college that will accept you is also important if you are thinking of a post-college education: like medicine, law, business, and so forth. These post-college professional schools will be *very* selective about who they admit. You'll need a college preparation that will get you into a good school after college, if that's what you decide to do.

Therefore, if colleges are looking for active and interesting people as well as excellent students, the person inside the student becomes significant. How do admissions officers find out about that person? Through extracurriculars and letters of recommendation.

Part 1: What's an "extra"?

Extracurricular activities, or "extras," for short, cover a wide range of school-related activities, such as athletics, music, forensics, the school newspaper, student government, and the many clubs that schools offer. Out-of-school activities count, too: scouting, 4-H, church groups, volunteer groups, and even your part-time job. Yes, jobs, too, are "extras." Anything you regularly do outside of classes, anything that takes time, commitment, energy, and intelligence, is considered an extra.

We've said that people who evaluate college applications usually want to discover who you are as a complete person, not just as a set of grades and SAT or ACT scores. Why is that?

What makes "extras" important?

Look at it this way. High grades, test scores, and academic awards tell a lot about you — that you are intelligent, diligent, focused, even determined and creative. However, they do not reveal your broader and deeper qualities: your personality or your character. If people who admit students to competitive colleges or who award scholarships looked only at transcripts, their decisions would be poor, indeed. And their colleges would be poorer for it. Good colleges want interesting, creative, energetic, and well-rounded students in their classrooms and on their campuses.

Brain power without strength of personality and character is not enough. And while students should develop both personality and character in the classroom, grades really tell only about organizing, managing, and gaining knowledge. That's why college admissions officers, scholarship committees, or directors of college honors programs look beyond your grades and test scores to the summary of extracurricular activities that you include in your college application.

In an extracurricular summary, students define themselves personally, highlighting qualities like leadership, enthusiasm, responsibility, respect for others, generosity, and the desire to expand their outlook on life. "Extras" help define you as a full person. They transform you from a black-and-white photo into a video presentation with background music and color commentary!

The student with a strong list of "extras" will always have the competitive edge when applying to competitive colleges. But don't misunderstand. "Extras" are not going to make up for average or inconsistent grades. However, when a student is applying for admission to any kind of competitive college — or for a scholarship, or a financial-aid award — a strong extracurricular profile is simply essential.

What is "strong"?

Strong doesn't mean that you must sign up for 14 clubs, play a sport every season, work a job 25 hours each week, plus do charity work and run for class president. A "packed" extracurricular resume will only make you look overwhelmed and rather unbelievable. Evaluators will realize that you couldn't do much for any single activity if you had to divide your time among so many. And with so many out-of-classroom activities, the first question someone reviewing your application will ask is, "*Did this student ever study?*"

At the other extreme, one "extra" is not enough. You are definitely much better off devoting your time to a few varied "extras" and really becoming involved in them. That way, college officials will easily recognize the *quality* of your involvement and dedication, rather than the length of your list. Also, you should have one "extra" that really stands out, one that shows you are truly remarkable and outstanding: for example, being a class officer, an outstanding athlete or member of the high school band/orchestra, or holding a leadership position in a club or organization.

Here's one last point about extracurricular activities. If you have a career goal in mind, look for "work extras" that relate to that goal. If you hope to become a physician, see what kind of work you can do as a volunteer or summer employee in a hospital or medical center. Think you want to go to law school after college? See if a law firm needs a student to help part-time. Engineering, accounting, finance, journalism? Ask your parents and family friends if anyone can introduce you to someone working in these fields. Go to see these people to find out more about working in these careers. In the process, you might find yourself a summer job that will give you a great career experience — as well as something you can put on your extracurricular "resume."

Another way that colleges examine the *student as a person* is to look at letters written by teachers and guidance counselors who know you. That's the topic of the next section.

Part 2: Why recommendations are important

Imagine you're applying to a competitive college. Name three teachers, counselors, or extracurricular advisers who know you well enough right now to write a detailed one-page recommendation for you.

1. _____
2. _____
3. _____

Letters of recommendation are written by people in your high school who know you very well — teachers, counselors, moderators, and directors of programs. They describe your excellent qualities as a person as well as a student. These letters are a traditional part of the college application and admissions process. While many colleges want only one recommendation from your academic counselor, really competitive and selective colleges usually want two. Sometimes three letters are needed if you are applying to a particular college and want to enroll in a certain program within the college — like an honors program or an exclusive area of study that accepts only small numbers of students. Even if you need only one recommendation, it could make a great deal of difference in reaching your college goals.

Like your extracurricular activities, recommendations describe you more fully as a person. They are the testimony of people who see you in comparison with many other students. By writing a letter of recommendation, a teacher or a guidance counselor who is impressed by your personal qualities can explain how you are special or outstanding. The letter writer can say that you have not only a remarkable mind but also traits that distinguish you from other students. For example, well-written recommendations can help convince college officials that you are creative, articulate and expressive (you can talk), motivated, respectful, friendly, generous, and honest — all things they can't see on your transcript.

Good recommendations are just as important as extracurricular activities in giving students a competitive edge. Both should be taken seriously. How do you take recommendations seriously? Just as you should choose your extras carefully and then work to develop your involvement, you should plan for letters of recommendation far ahead of the time you will need them. Remember that you will begin applying to colleges early in your senior year. Therefore, your recommendations will come from people who know you well by the end of your junior year. Understanding this should motivate you to be a conscientious, college smart student who gets to know your teachers as soon as you enter high school.

Remember that any one of your teachers or counselors is a potential recommender for you. So whether you are in a classroom or in a school office, you should conduct yourself to impress these people you might be asking for a recommendation later on. And when the time comes to ask for recommendations, never just hand over a recommendation form or a note with a college address. Make an appointment to see the recommender and talk about your college plans.

At the same time, hand over your summary of extracurricular activities, a copy of the college application essay(s) that you've written, your ACT or SAT reports, and a list of the colleges in which you are interested. A recommender can use this information to help compose and shape a full and detailed recommendation.

Finally, don't let anyone tell you that recommendations and extracurricular resumes are *"not that important – nobody looks at them anyway."* Even if college officials ignore them (and some do), that's not your concern. When admissions officers take the time to examine these items, they can make all the difference in the world in the decision-making process. When you want to get into the colleges that are just right for you, never be careless about your applications and the details and procedures they require.

What a letter of recommendation says

Do you wonder what people say in a really good letter of recommendation? The letter should contain the following information.

Credentials of the letter writer

- Who is the recommender? Teacher, counselor?
- How does the recommender know the student, and for how long?
- What are the recommender's credentials? College degrees? Years of teaching? Teaching what courses? At what schools?
- How would the recommender rate your high school's college-preparation curriculum compared to others?

- Over the years, how many students has the recommender taught?
- How would the student rank among all students the recommender has taught?
- Does the student have a good reputation among other faculty? Other students?
- How does the recommender know the student other than through class performance? Advising sessions? Casual conversation? Formal appointments? School activities?
- Does the recommender feel knowledgeable about the student's personality and character?

The student as a person

- Personality: Is the student mature, confident, determined; optimistic, realistic, open-minded; energetic, generous, friendly; serious about education; considerate of others?
- Character: Is the student honest, respectful, trustworthy, responsible, ethical, compassionate?
- How has the student demonstrated various qualities of personality and character?

The student as a student

- What does the student think about a college education? Well-thought-out and well-planned? Excited about it?
- If the student is applying to very competitive colleges, does the recommender know the student's reasons for choosing these colleges?
- Does the student get strong encouragement and support from family?
- Does the recommender know what areas of study the student is interested in?
- Why does the recommender feel the student will be successful in college?
- Does the recommender know what plans the student has *after* college?
- Does the student have particular career or professional goals?
- Where does the recommender see the student in ten years?

In asking for a recommendation, as a courtesy, you could give the recommender a copy of this recommendation profile to use as a guide.

Listen to Dr. Bob —

Why you should practice this Strategy for college

A recent survey shows that the grades of college-bound high school students are higher than they have ever been in history. Is this good news? Not for the student who is applying to competitive or selective colleges. Why? First, here are the statistics on high school grade point averages for students enrolling in colleges:

- 24% have *A* or *A+* averages
- 24% have *A-* averages
- 21% have *B+* averages

Source: *The American Freshman: National Norms for Fall 2004,* American Council on Education, Published by the American Council on Education and University of California at Los Angeles Higher Education Research Institute.

Because so many students are getting grades that are so high, transcripts don't always help college admissions officers very much in differentiating applicants. If you are an *A* student, you have to think that many other applicants are also *A* students. What will make you stand out? Well, make sure you prepare for those SATs and ACTs. They're really important. What else? Make sure you have an impressive summary of extracurricular activities along with substantial recommendations. In both cases, you have to take steps to make sure that these factors in your application help you stand out from the crowd.

Here's another tip about applying to competitive colleges. Find out from your guidance counselor if any students from your high school are currently attending these colleges. If so, as part of your application, you might mention this fact.

PSST! Scan the highlights and think ahead. Think about your current extracurriculars. Think about your relationships with your teachers. How many could answer these recommendation questions about you? Are you in good shape?

Up close and personal
Sara: What her recommendation didn't say.

Remember Sara from Strategy 4? She had perfect ACT scores and ranked #1 in her class, but she couldn't get past the interviews for top colleges. Her inability to talk hurt her, and because her teacher recommendations were neutral, they hurt her, too. Let me explain.

At my university, I worked closely with the Admissions Office, so I looked at student applications almost daily. When university officers review recommendations, they look at what is written — *and what is not written.*

Neutral letters will say something like *"While I do not know this student personally, she was in my _____ class and earned a _____."* Such language tells admissions counselors that this is a passive student who, after three years in high school and many teachers, cannot produce a truly personal letter of recommendation. What the letter actually says is that this student may have earned high grades but failed to distinguish himself or herself from other students.

In other words, what the teacher DIDN'T say was a story in itself. Colleges wanted to hear that Sara not only was bright and capable but also actively participated in discussions … that she made the class more interesting for other students … and that the class was better because she was in it.

Sara's teachers said none of these things. When teachers write recommendations, they praise students wherever possible because teachers know colleges are interested in that kind of personal information. When the top colleges looked at Sara's letters of recommendation, they saw what was missing. Sara's grades, class rank, and test scores were very similar to those of many other students. Nothing distinguished Sara from other good applicants.

When you're aiming at a top college, your competition (other applicants) looks just like you. Always be thinking, planning, and working to distinguish yourself. Make your education more than going to class and earning grades. Extend that achievement and effort to significant things that you do outside of your classes. Sara wasn't the "complete" or "distinguished" student she might have been. So the top colleges passed her by. They had plenty of other remarkable students to choose from.

Extracurricular activities show colleges that you are intent on growing and expanding your experience both inside and outside of the classroom. Exceptional colleges want not only talented, but highly motivated, students. Letters of recommendation may make a difference in earning you a place in your "special college," so you should try to impress the people who will write those letters. Both extracurricular activities and letters of recommendation will help admissions officers make the right decisions about your educational future.

Dean's commentary

As a college dean, each time I had an appointment with a student, I would first look at the student's file, and that included his or her college application and recommendations. Too many times, the recommendations said little more than, *"This is a real good student who really wants to attend your college."* My colleagues at very competitive colleges would say that they, too, received a good number of poor recommendations.

Perhaps high school counselors and teachers are asked to write too many recommendations, so they don't have time to compose good letters. But I suspect another reason, too: The students who needed the recommendations are often careless and simply handed over a recommendation form at the last minute with no conversation or background materials, like college application essays or ACT or SAT reports.

When given "last-minute" notice and without other information, recommenders naturally lose both energy and creativity in preparing recommendations.

As a college smart student, that won't happen to you. You have already built a relationship with your recommender, so he or she can speak specifically about you as a person. Your recommender can write about your special interest in a particular course, your leadership in class discussions, your care in following a Personal Study Schedule, your motivation to earn high grades, and your serious drive to succeed with your education. Are you hearing any bells ringing? Do all of these qualities sound like things you've heard in earlier Strategies? Of course. Is it all starting to come together for you? Are you beginning to see how the Strategies work for you on many levels?

Finally, it's true that some colleges might not care much about the recommendations they request — they may use them only when making difficult admissions decisions. (You never know exactly how colleges evaluate your application.) But you must treat recommendations and extracurriculars as counting significantly in the admissions process. You don't know what role they will play for you. So as far as you're concerned, believe that they are as important as grades and test scores, and give them the attention they require. **RU READY?**

I stay on target to achieve my dreams!

Setting goals — getting to the top. What a view!
(All about your aims, ambitions, aspirations, desires, and hopes.)

In a survey, new college freshmen were asked to comment on how interesting they found their last year of high school. Almost half said they were frequently bored. Only 25% of college-bound high school seniors talked to teachers about their courses, and only 11% spent 7 or more hours a week studying.

Now compare those "boredom" statistics to these:

- *40% of students arrive at college needing remedial work. 25% of these students need "substantial" help — many in several subjects.*
- *Only 50% of new college students have taken adequate college-prep courses.*
- *Only 36% (about 1 in 3) of college students complete a degree in four years.*
- *25% of college freshmen do not return to the college where they started (some do not return to school at all).*

High school boredom seems to seriously harm students in college.

Part 1: Goals for combatting boredom now

BOOORRRRING!!!! (That's "boring" with emphasis.)

How about you? Do you find school boring? Do you wish you could skip school altogether and just start life? If so, this final Strategy is for you. It's about avoiding boredom — academic and otherwise. It's about adding interest, challenge, and enthusiasm to what you might consider your "dreary and monotonous" school days.

How? You begin by bringing to school a sense of the future. You link your school days to your goals: what you might like to be or to do. Don't say, *"Here's another boring Tuesday."* Tuesday — and every other day in high school — connects you to your future in college and in life. How you use each day builds your future.

This Strategy will show you how focusing on goals shakes off boredom. Boredom is dangerous, and it's the reason that thousands of students entering college need "remediation" — despite their good high school grades.

Where the boredom comes from

In grade school, you didn't have to set goals, because your teachers set them for you, telling you exactly what to do. *"Today we are going to listen carefully to the story so we can answer questions later." "This afternoon, we are going to practice writing neatly." "Now, we're going to play a game to prepare for tomorrow's test."* Elementary school was a time of close teacher-student relationships. Teachers made learning exciting. They helped and encouraged you. Your teacher moved from desk to desk, either congratulating you on a job well done or helping you understand if you were confused. In short, your teacher worked with you to reach learning goals each day. Those were the "good old days." The emphasis is on "old," because things are quite different now.

In middle school, that close teacher-student relationship suddenly changed. You had several teachers, and you moved from classroom to classroom. The teacher spent most of class time explaining concepts. To succeed, you had to set goals for yourself — everything from paying attention in class, to completing homework thoughtfully, to handing in assignments on time, to studying carefully for tests. What's more, once you set these goals, it was up to you to MAKE THE EFFORT TO REACH THEM. That's the important second step.

Without your teachers' individual attention and support, you may have found that some subjects became harder for you than others. You found yourself on your own, wrestling with them. If you were a student who lacked determination, your first thought was just to give up on a hard subject. However, the educational system expected you to be mature enough to work independently. YOU were supposed to encourage yourself, saying, *"I know math is tough for me, so I'll have to work harder to get it."* Or, *"It's difficult doing all this reading and writing, but I'll stick with it because I need these skills."* For some of you, this worked; for others, it failed.

For those of you who decided to "give up" on a hard subject, then what happened? Your interest in the subject quickly dropped off. You no longer liked it. In class, you fell behind, and the less you knew, the harder the subject became. That's when boredom set in — and boredom can be fatal. Think "fatal" is an overly dramatic word? It's not. Giving up on a subject affects not just your grades *but your entire future.* Don't believe it? Read on!

How boredom wrecks your future

Let's say that math is harder for you than other subjects, so you decide "you're just not good at math." It takes too much work. You stop studying it, and that feels great. Now let's look at the other consequences of your decision.

- You can no longer be an engineer of any kind. (No bridges or buildings in your future.)

- You can't work in any scientific field. (No revolutionary discoveries for you.)

- Most medical careers are out for you. (You won't be doing any life-saving procedures.)

- You've eliminated many careers related to the natural sciences. (You won't help the world become clean again.)

- A large number of careers in business are out for you, too. (What would Donald Trump say about that!)

Simply put, a negative attitude (boredom) toward math suddenly closes doors to many careers.

"Wait a minute," you say, *"that can't be right."* Yes, it is. Whether or not you realized what you were doing, you did it. You were thinking about your comfort level today, and you forgot all about the many tomorrows that are the rest of your life. When you live only in the present, you forget about the future. Instead of just studying harder in math and math-related courses, you sit back, relax — and watch many opportunities for your future fade away. In short, because you wouldn't set new learning goals for yourself, like working harder in math, you became a restricted, limited person.

The same thing happens if you "give up" on verbal skills, reading, writing, listening, and talking:

- You can no longer be a teacher of any kind. (Even if you would love to teach algebra or biology, you won't have the skills to explain what you know to others.)

- You can't work in any communications field. (No job as a news anchor or sports reporter. You can't write Web sites or ads for cell phones.)

- Being a psychologist is out for you. (You have to be able to talk easily to people and help them understand their problems.)

- You've eliminated many careers in the corporate world. (Major requirements in business are listening, talking to many kinds of people, and making yourself understood: writing memos, reports, and proposals. It's not anything like instant messaging.)

- No work in politics helping a candidate run for the senate. (These aides have to be good listeners, clear writers, and very confident speakers who relay and analyze information.)

Excitement, not boredom

What if you looked at a hard subject the way some people look at highly competitive sports? It's a challenge to be in a tournament and play the difficult teams. Athletes who win tournaments are proud of their hard work and accomplishments. Why not see difficult subjects as an opportunity, the same kind of challenge? A chance to learn new things that might be exciting and interesting. Hard work leads to accomplishment. You feel good about yourself because you conquered something that was not easy for you. That's what makes you proud.

Think long-term

When you give up on a hard subject, you change your whole life by locking doors to many professions, some you didn't even know existed. You have also set a terrible pattern of behavior for yourself. When something is hard, you don't do it. Think of what that means to you, not just as a college student, but as someone who hopes for certain careers and jobs that are personally and financially rewarding.

What do you think will happen if you want to become a doctor, a lawyer, or an accountant, but you just can't manage certain parts of the admissions test? What do you plan to say to an admissions officer? *"I'm just not good at standardized tests. Could you admit me anyway?"* (Get used to people looking at you with expressions of *"Are you kidding me?"*) Or can you imagine the reaction when you say to a future boss *"I'm not good at that — you better give the project to someone else."* (Don't look for any promotions or salary increases in the near future.)

Without the ability, intelligence, and motivation to set and achieve new goals each day of your life, you cannot grow and evolve. Don't think only for the moment. Think long-term. Oprah Winfrey says, *"The big secret in life is that there is no big secret. Whatever your goal, you can get there only if you are willing to work."*

The left-brain/right-brain trap

In high school, students who don't develop a self-encouraging, goal-setting attitude begin to say things like, *"Writing is hard — I'm just not good at it,"* as if somehow they were born without writing ability.

As early as grade school, many students and their parents are told about "right-brained and left-brained learning," and the result can be disastrous. The right/left-brain theory explains that people can be divided into two groups of learners. If you are "left-brained," you are good at math and solving problems. If you are "right-brained," you are good at language, reading, and writing.

But people misunderstand the concept. They think that their "brain styles" block learning a subject. NOT SO. The truth is that the right/left-brain theory refers only to a person's *style or manner* of learning, not his or her ability. There's no reason that the left-brained student can't learn "right-brained" subjects, or the reverse. When you decide to give up on a subject, it isn't a matter of "cannot"; it's a matter of "will not."

The great value of balanced knowledge

When students simply give up on one type of academic subject, they weaken their overall strength. Want some examples?

Brilliant engineers who cannot write or speak to others to explain their designs or projects hurt their opportunities for professional growth. The journalist who cannot understand economics limits what he or she can write about. The doctor who studied "only" science courses cannot communicate very well with patients or other doctors.

Deciding too early in life about "what you are good at" or "which courses you will work for" can dramatically limit your life. So as long as you are in school, work not just for depth of knowledge, but balanced and broad knowledge, too.

In the here-and-now

A well-balanced education with a consistently high academic record will earn you competitive scores on the SAT and ACT, which require both language and math/science skills. Ultimately, your excellent grades and scores get you into the college that's right for you. What's more, that college will give you great scholarships because you worked hard to develop BOTH sides of your brain. Then your college education will give you more opportunities for your future than you could ever imagine.

Part 2: Goals for your future life

You have to look at learning and see it for what it is. Learning is about meeting goals — and every time you meet Tuesday's goal or Friday's goal, you are going places. You meet small goals this week, and when you do, you are bringing yourself closer to a more distant place: your future. You work toward larger goals by reaching for (and sometimes wrestling with) smaller goals. Each new level of learning opens new possibilities for your future.

Learn about yourself

Are you a goal setter? *Check any that apply to you.*

_____ No, I live from day to day. Life's too unpredictable.

_____ I set goals, but I don't usually keep them. They fizzle out.

_____ I don't think goals work. They never have for me.

_____ I always tell myself, "*This year, I'll do better.*" That's a goal, isn't it?

_____ Who has time to set goals?

_____ Only organized people have goals. I'm a creative freethinker.

_____ I set some goals, but I don't know if they're the right ones.

_____ I set goals, but they get lost in the hundred other things in my life.

_____ I'm a goal-setter from way back. Goals keep me motivated.

What about your future? Whether or not you have goals from day to day, semester to semester, or year to year, what about the BIG GOAL — a career or profession? *Check any that apply to you.*

_____ I think about my future, mostly daydreams filled with huge successes.

_____ I frequently talk to adults to learn about their jobs and careers.

_____ I trust in fate. Things always work out, right?

_____ A few careers interest me, but I don't know much about them.

_____ I try to think about what I want to be, but it's all so overwhelming.

_____ I talk regularly to my teachers and counselors about colleges, careers, and jobs.

_____ It's all so scary that right now. I'm just avoiding it. I'll think about it later.

Strategies, goals, and graduating from college on time

If you don't regularly set goals, you need to learn how. Setting goals combats boredom. What kind of goals? Both large and small — from small goals like a high grade in your next physics quiz, to larger goals like increasing your grade point average, to really big goals like graduating from college. Yes, GRADUATING from college. If you think just *getting into* college is your goal, you're mistaken. *Succeeding* in college and *graduating* are your goals, and not too many students are reaching them these days.

How important is being a college smart student? Take a look at college graduation rates. Right now, the graduation rate is very poor. Students in colleges and universities across the nation are taking extra years to finish their degrees. Many fail to earn degrees at all. It's hard to believe that these are the same students who earned *As* in high school. Here are the facts:

- **Only about 1 out of 3 students (37%) earns a college degree in 4 years.**
- **In 5 or 6 years, that percentage rises to only 63%.**
- **In other words, nearly 40% take longer than 6 years or NEVER earn a degree — researchers stop tracking numbers after 6 years.**

Could things be worse? Unfortunately, yes. In the past few years, graduation rates have continued to fall. College students who DO manage to graduate are taking longer and longer to finish degrees, and that means they are spending more and more money.

What's the problem?

There's more involved in college success than your ACT/SAT scores and your grade point average. Success has to do with different kinds of abilities: your ability to manage your courses, your time, and yourself. In addition, your self-encouragement and how well you set and reach goals will make all the difference.

Announcement for all those going to college:
Pack up your goals and take them with you to campus.
You'll need them to graduate.

Learn about yourself

List some important long-term goals for yourself (like college, career, financial reward, personal relationships).

1. _____
2. _____
3. _____
4. _____
5. _____

Students who are not focused on distant goals put off this kind of thinking. Plus, they don't begin seriously thinking about college until fall of their senior year. They especially haven't thought much about why they are really going to college. (Mostly, it's because everybody else is going.)

Even worse, they haven't considered how much high school prepares them for college. They don't think about how specific high school courses will relate to college courses. For example —

- Many college courses require research papers of some length. What if you don't take college-prep courses, and you've never had to write an essay more than one page (double spaced)? That puts you at a great disadvantage.

- Many colleges require competence in a foreign language. What if you dropped Spanish after your second year of high school?

- Many colleges set a standard for math ability. Plus, many non-science areas of study require math or computer competence. If you decided to "forget about" math, you might have a problem completing a degree in these academic areas.

Did you ever stop to think that each phase of your education — elementary, secondary, college, post-college — lays a foundation for the next? Or that each year forms a basis for the following year? Or that each day has meaning for the next? If not, you're in trouble. If you haven't thought about these ideas, you probably don't set goals for yourself.

Getting from here to the end of the semester

When I ask students to name some goals for a new semester, as you would expect, the first thing most students tell me is that their main goal is *to get high final grades. To procrastinate less* comes in a close second.

Granted, keeping an eye on final grades at the start of the semester is important. But how do you make those final grades happen? They don't occur because you "really, really hope they will." There's a lot of time between the beginning and the end of the semester. What keeps you going from day to day? Smaller goals that you can control, achieve, and evaluate every day. So I ask students to set DAILY goals: for example, study all courses every day, work with a schedule, stay organized to relieve stress, and talk to professors regularly. These smaller goals are called short-term goals.

Short- and long-term goals work together.

Short-term goals get you to your long-term goals. That may seem obvious, but students often lose sight of the connection between the two. If you don't keep your larger purpose (long-term goals) clear in your mind, you can lose your determination to do your daily job as a student. On the other hand, if you don't do your daily jobs (short-term goals), you won't achieve your long-term goal.

Be college smart. True, students need to keep their eye on the long-term goals, but they get there by taking care of daily tasks. It's a one-step-at-a-time process. The distant goals are your destination; the short-term goals are the means to get you there. It's as simple as that.

Let's say you're studying more and better each day (short-term goal). You're sharpening your intellect to reach two long-term goals: high final grades and high SAT/ACT scores. Getting high grades and high scores will help you with an even longer-term goal: admission to a high-quality college. Such a college will open the door to careers or professions, your *ultimate* long-term goal.

Hopes, dreams, strategies, and goals

Some students focus only on their distant goals. *I want to be a famous architect who designs buildings that last forever. I want to own a big company and have a lot of people working for me. I want to be like Bill Gates — earn a fortune at an early age and spend the rest of my life giving away my money to help people.* These are dreams, and there's nothing wrong with them. We all need them. But we must not mistake dreams for goals. Successful people will tell you that the most important part of setting goals is creating the strategies and plans to achieve them.

You have to understand that hopes, dreams, strategies, and goals can get confused. Of course, they're interconnected. They are like the strands of a rope. They all work together. But the strands are separate. Don't mistake dreams for strategies. Dreams show you your destination. Hopes are your motivation. Strategies are the steps that get you to your goals. So occasionally, you must untwist the strands and see them separately.

Remind yourself that what you do today as a student affects you tomorrow. What you do this semester affects you next year. Next year directly affects you two, three, and four years from now.

Be college smart. *"What"* goals won't get you there. You need to have a *"how" strategy.* Here are some examples to help you get the point:

What: Discovering a career is one of my major long-term goals.

How: Taking a career-interest test, meeting someone who works in my field of interest, or interning in a company, hospital, or business might help point me in the right career direction.

What: Raise my grade in History.

How: Increase the amount of time I give History in my study schedule.

What: Improve my talking skills.

How: Make a serious effort to talk to teachers, counselors, and adults.

What: Master the 12 Strategies

How: Add at least one new Strategy to my routine each week until I've added them all. I'll begin right NOW!

Your goals are private.

Setting goals for yourself, long-term or short-term, can be scary. Why? There are so many goals to choose from. And what if you fail? Maybe it's the fear of failing that keeps you from setting goals. There's also the fear of looking foolish if you fail. What will your friends say? What will your family say? Unless you're going to publish your goals in the school newspaper, your goals are private and personal. Talk to friends about them as much or little as you want — or not at all.

However, know this about goals from the start:

- You'll reach some goals more easily than others.

- You won't always succeed.

- Most goals need to be reshaped as you go along.

- You have great freedom — you can change your mind, you can change your strategies to succeed, you can even change your outlook on life.

But one thing is certain. You must learn how to set goals for yourself for tomorrow, for next week, as well as the distant future. You must make achieving goals part of your regular personal routine. Setting and reaching goals is a life skill. If you don't start practicing now, you won't understand how to do it later — even when your survival depends on it, like meeting the demands of your college courses.

Learning how to set goals and to make plans to reach them is as important as learning any or all of your high school subjects. Remember when I told you earlier that learning *how* to learn is as important as *what* you learn? A major part of that *how* is setting and achieving goals. The 12 Strategies give you the *hows* in reaching goals. More on that in a minute.

Use the **My Goals Tracker** at the end of this strategy to get started.

Your educational mountain — a Mt. Everest of knowledge

Do you remember that earlier in this guidebook, I compared your education to climbing a mountain, the top of the mountain being a college diploma? Climbing, like learning, is exciting and requires special skills. Unlike floating lazily on a raft down a river, mountain climbing is not something to be taken casually. Mountain climbing can be very thrilling, but climbers must keep their wits about them at all times.

The climb gets harder as the mountain grows steeper. As you, the climber, move up the mountain in stages, each new leg of your journey prepares you for the next. While the ultimate goal may be to reach the summit, all along the way, climbers are busy *setting short-term goals to get them to the next stage on the mountain.* You must continually grow and prepare for the next stage of your climb. You must keep developing as a student.

By now, you know that real academic success doesn't "just happen." You have to work at learning. Like the mountain climber, a student must be intelligent, clever, strong, careful, determined, and courageous. Now, in *high* school, you're *higher* up the mountain. You cannot afford to be careless or bored. As an educational climber, you're being asked to act more independently and develop strength. You do that by using the 12 Strategies. They show you *how* to achieve your daily and long-term goals:

- Every class is important: Come in "processing mode"......................Strategies #1 and 2

- Study requires time and effort..Strategies #2, 3, and 7

- Controlling your time means scheduling..Strategy #8

- Time should be used productively because you have many things to do and only so many hours in a day........................Strategies #2 and 8

- Talking makes you independent, involves you in the learning process, and earns you good recommendations.......Strategies #4, 5, 6, and 11

- Evaluating your progress shows you how well your effort is meeting the challenge of each course ....Strategies #9 and 10

- Tracking tells you when to adjust your approach....................................Strategy #10

- Extracurriculars help your college application process ....Strategy #11

- Goals keep you moving forward..Strategy #12

Use this guidebook throughout high school. Things you do — or don't do — every day affect your future, both near and far. Master the 12 Strategies now to prepare for the final ascent: the college years. What you do now will determine if you will be one of the college students who actually graduates — on time and in an area of study that makes you happy.

And what happens if you don't take your high school education seriously? If you don't understand how it prepares you for the college stage of the mountain? You'll end up circling the mountain without gaining any ground. You'll become a college student who doesn't graduate.

You can get to the summit!

Find a direction. Plan how to get there. Do the work. Stick to your plan — or adjust it because you've found a new direction. Don't give up. You're in control. You can do this. This is life. Your life. Your education. And you're in charge of it. So take charge of it.

You have so many opportunities, but you have to pursue them. Remember all that independence and control you're looking for? You have it. You just don't recognize it. Your life is in your own hands, not anybody else's. Just like the college smart climber, you're creating the footholds, planting your axe, staying alert to changing conditions, and choosing the path up this mountain. You plan, adjust, replan, and adjust again. You're crafting your own future. How's that for freedom? Every day is a step closer to your goals, a step backward, or no step at all. It's all up to you!

By now, you know that you should try to be good at *everything* in high school so that you don't disqualify yourself from career paths you haven't yet discovered. So take courses of "substance" and remember what you learn. Then, in college, you'll discover an area of study that really interests you. You want to *choose* a career that is exciting to you, not *settle* for something because your background disqualifies you from other careers.

The more you learn and do in high school, the more options you have — and the better prepared you are to try anything. That doesn't mean you won't change your mind once or twice, but at least you will have the opportunity to try different career paths. The view from the top of the mountain should be a bright and wide vista. What you do now determines how bright and wide that vista will be.

College is a big goal in your life right now, and an important one. Place it right in front of you and work on it every day in every class. As a college smart student, you become a motivated student and an interesting person. Boredom disappears. In its place, you discover new challenges, fresh excitement, and opportunities for academic growth and creativity. The key is setting and achieving goals — goals that define your dreams and hopes.

This is your future!

Listen to Dr. Bob

And keep listening at his Web site....
www.rureallyready4college.com or www.areyoureallyreadforcollege.com

When you have children or nieces or nephews of your own, what story will you tell them about your education? For the Typical and Clueless Students, the story will sound something like, *"Well, first I went to kindergarten at a school in …. Then I went to grade school at …. After that …."* For the young listeners, this will certainly be a bedtime story that will put them to sleep.

On the other hand, for College Smart Students like you, the story will be exciting — an adventure filled with intrigue, suspense, and thrilling revelations. Why? Because it will be a story of setting goals and reaching them, finding new ones, and using your imagination, creativity, and enthusiasm at every turn.

You will be able to tell young listeners about how your plans to be an aeronautical engineer almost disappeared when you started to take calculus — it was the hardest course you ever took. But you didn't give up. You expanded your study schedule, went to review sessions, and regularly talked to your teacher. You finished the semester with an *A* in the course. You can tell your young listeners how proud you were of that *A* grade because it was so tough to get. You can also tell them that conquering calculus gave you the confidence to try other hard things. Calculus opened up a whole new world for you, and you could handle it!

That *A* set the stage for your college math courses, which led to your degree in engineering from a very prestigious college. Now that's what you call really reaching a goal!

Or what about that art course you took? A lot of students took it just to fill a requirement slot and get an easy *A*. But you had always liked art and drawing, and this "easy" course became a way for you to discover your artistic talents. You learned not only about basic drawing, but design, as well. Computerized design was really interesting to you, and this knowledge ultimately gave you a broader view of your career as an engineer. In fact, you can say that you still use knowledge from that course in solving engineering problems.

Or let's change the example. As a College Smart college graduate, you could tell young listeners about the time you wrote your first research paper in high school. You thought it was going to be just like those short papers in middle school — just longer. (How's that for logic?) You spent several days trying to figure out how to get started. Should you research a topic first and then find an idea to write about? Or should you find the idea first and then try to research it? (You hadn't listened very well to the instructions about the assignment in class.) After several days of spinning your wheels, with the due date looming ever closer, *you broke down and went to see the teacher*. You'd never talked with a teacher about an assignment before, which shows how desperate you were at the time.

To your surprise, the teacher gave you all kinds of tips that pointed you in the right direction. It was a good thing, too, because this was a much harder paper than you had thought it was at first.

You learned so much from this teacher that you found you liked talking about how to write and writing assignments. Every time you asked the teacher to translate the red marks on your pages, you learned more about how to make language work for you. In fact, you found that you liked writing. This teacher was a turning point for you. As a result of the teacher's coaching, you now earn your living as a professional writer, and you love it. At the time, you hadn't given a career in writing a second thought.

The moral of the story for your young listeners is that every course is important. Each has both obvious and hidden qualities. But while your education may have many parts, intellectual achievement comes to you only when you truly understand how the parts form a WHOLE, how every course you take is connected to all the others. With that understanding, you'll be successful in college. But more than that, you will ultimately realize that you are always a student — whether or not you are in a classroom. The best and most successful people are those who love learning and love being a student. Life always has something to teach us, and we always have to be ready and able to learn. Be college smart for the rest of your life, and you'll love every minute of it.

 PSST! These highlights about goals and how to reach them tell a story that can change your life. Read them over and over again to keep you focused and really succeeding throughout high school.

And bring this book to college! By rereading all the highlights and following their advice, you can avoid being a member of that nearly 40% who never graduate from college. Plus, you'll graduate in a field that you like, not that you can manage. This will make all the difference in your life.

Up close and personal
(Your name), a College Smart Student

In previous Strategies, I have told you stories, *"up close and personal,"* about students with assorted successes and failures. This final story is about you. As a college smart student, each day, you make the most of the Strategies described in this guidebook.

Because you're college smart, a great many students look at you with envy. They say you're "really smart" — you make classes more interesting because of your comments and questions. And, oh yes, they also like your friendly personality. You're fun to talk to.

Of course, you know that your success as a student isn't as natural as being tall or having red hair. You've worked hard to be the kind of student you are. Plus, you continue to work harder each day because you know that you will be a student for the rest of your life: always learning new things, always solving problems, always creating ways to better understand and manage your life and your many roles in it. For you, school is practice for life, and when you get there, that's a "contest" you want to win.

You may not always love every minute of every school day, but because you have decided that learning is a challenge, you approach each class, each day, as something like an athletic event you're determined to win! You're the competitive type. You like challenges, both big and small. For you, nothing is better than having a new goal to achieve.

Today, for example, is a typical day for you. In the morning, after a good night's sleep and nutritious breakfast, you look at your Personal Study Schedule to remind yourself of the many things your day holds for you. Let's see.

- You have a quiz in math – you're ready for that.

- There are homework assignments in English and History – you did those carefully last night. (These are your favorite courses, but they're hard because they're Advanced Placement courses.)

- You are up to date on your Spanish vocabulary and tense endings.

- You're really looking forward to Biology because your class is going on a field trip today. You did extra reading for that.

- Oh, yes, you are really proud of the drawing you did for art class.

You're more than ready to face the day.

Looking ahead this week, you don't want to forget about your appointment with your counselor. You're bringing in information about three more colleges you might apply to. Oh, and remember to sign up for that Career Fair next week, and that College Fair next month.

As you head for your first class, you think about the new material your teacher will present. As always, you have read ahead, so you're prepared, but you've a question to ask. In the classroom, you head for your favorite seat, right up front in the second row, so that your eyes and mind always stay focused on your teacher.

Before class begins, you say "hi" to your friends, and then as the class settles, you scan the notes you wrote last night as you read the textbook. Flipping through the pages of your notebook, you notice your **Grade Tracker** for this course. Nice to see all those high grades from the last six weeks. It's just the boost you need to focus on today's class.

During class, you take notes and ask questions whenever you don't understand something. The teacher appreciates you, and so do the other students, because you ask good questions that they might be reluctant to ask.

After class, you approach your teacher to ask about a due date for an upcoming assignment. You do this without hesitation because you talk to all your teachers regularly. You learned long ago that communication is one of the keys to your academic success. You know that exchanging ideas is what learning is all about.

As you move from class to class, you feel exhilarated because new ideas and concepts are stimulating. When you are learning, you are feeling great. You don't understand those students (some are your friends) who are always complaining. *"I totally hate that class." "Man, is that teacher ever boring." "I can't wait to get home after school and forget about all this junk."* Well, everyone has opinions; you just prefer looking on the bright side of school.

You're already thinking about doing your assignments and studying after school. You didn't always feel like planning your study time, not until you learned how to make a Personal Study Schedule. Now that you've blocked out study time as well as recreation time, you find you can do everything: from listening to music to playing with your dog. Having a Study Schedule actually keeps you from over-scheduling and gives you more time to do almost everything you want.

You watch your friends who do everything in a haphazard way. One thing you've noticed is that they study less and less and complain about being "overworked" more and more. They all need Personal Study Schedules!

For you, there's nothing like your private study place, your room. When you're here, no one disturbs you. Your friends know when to call and email you — even your family has learned to respect your study time. You have a great study table with a comfortable chair. You can spread everything out.

Each night, you do your homework assignments, and you study all of your courses, even those without "homework" or an upcoming test. You write everything down. Your notebooks are like an academic diary where you record everything: class notes, outlines of textbook chapters, memory charts, and lists.

You don't have specific homework for a couple of your courses, so you review old material and read ahead. You make sure to watch the clock because you are dedicated to a certain amount of study time each day.

School, school, school; study, study, study. Is that all you do or think about? Far from it. Because you keep to your study schedule, without fail, you actually have more free time than your friends. You still can watch your favorite TV show or surf the Web. You have a great part-time job on the weekends to make some spending money and add to your college fund.

You play tennis during one semester and run track in another. Keeping in shape keeps your mind sharp. And you work as a volunteer one Sunday a month. Bored? You don't know the meaning of the word.

So you must be the perfect student, right? Well, not quite. You may earn mostly *A*s, and your teachers look forward to writing letters of recommendation for you. But you want to get into a college that is in the *US News* Top 100 list, and that means some high SAT and ACT scores. Standardized tests, for you, mean serious preparation. You've taken both tests as a sophomore, so you know that you must really work hard to get ready for these tests.

When your day ends and you go to bed, you have a great sense of accomplishment. You're another day closer to college, another day closer to your future.

This is you. Up close and personal. Isn't it a great feeling when you have it all together? **RU READY?**

My Goals —
to be *really* ready for college:

	Goals & actual grades by grading period							
	1		**2**		**3**		**4**	
Classes I'm taking this semester:	Goal	Actual	Goal	Actual	Goal	Actual	Goal	Actual
1.								
2.								
3.								
4.								
5.								
6.								
	GPA		GPA		GPA		GPA	

These are my short-term goals for the semester: + = Good   ✓ = Okay   O = Needs Work

		Grading period			
	Goal	**1**	**2**	**3**	**4**
In class (Daily)	Follow my Personal Study Schedule daily				
	Listen carefully in every class				
	Take good class notes				
	Contribute to class discussions				
	Ask intelligent questions in class				
	Record all grades in Grade Tracker				
Study time (Daily)	Complete homework carefully				
	Study each course daily				
	Read and outline textbooks				
	Use study devices (note cards, outlines, memory lists)				
	Do extra math or science problems				
	Read ahead in all courses				
	Rewrite class notes				
	Rewrite papers and written assignments				
	Study ahead for tests				
	Review all graded tests and assignments				
	Start assignments before due date				
	Record all grades in my Grade Tracker				
	Maintain or increase grades in all courses				
Planning ahead (Monthly)	Talk about my progress with teachers				
	Talk to counselor about academic progress				
	Talk about college to teachers, counselors				
	Check admissions standards				
	Get information about careers				

**So that I remember why all of my short-term goals are important, these are my long-term goals:

1. Colleges I'm going to apply to				
2. GPA I need to get into my desired colleges				
3. SAT/ACT scores I need to get into my desired colleges				
4. Careers I want to pursue				

**These are the Strategies you are going to make part of your days.
These are the Strategies that will help you reach your goals—
*and make your dreams come true.***

Strategy 1   How, exactly, to "use your head"

Strategy 2   Your study place

Strategy 3   The first two weeks

Strategy 4   Knowing how to talk

Strategy 5   Talking to teachers

Strategy 6   Talking with your guidance counselor

Strategy 7   Studying vs. homework

Strategy 8   Creating a schedule

Strategy 9   All about tests

Strategy 10   Tracking grades

Strategy 11   Extracurricular activities and recommendations, too

Strategy 12   Setting goals

A look at you, a College Smart student

As you come to the end of this guidebook, I hope you understand how important it is to start practicing the 12 Strategies NOW, not later. Whether you are four years or four weeks away from college, whether you're starting a new semester or in the middle of one, your primary goal should be to make these Strategies a regular part of your days. Remember, we're talking about your future now, and nothing should stand in the way of realizing that future.

I want you to imagine yourself as a college smart student. What makes you college smart? Here are the essentials.

You keep your goals in mind. When? At the start of each semester. At the start of each new course. In fact, at the start of each new school day, you are thinking about goals — small and big. Every quiz grade, every final grade, every grade point average signals that you're learning more and more, better and better. As a student preparing for college, you can say, *"I'm college smart. I reach my goals."* As college moves closer, you are also setting larger college-related goals (where to go and why) so you will be absolutely college smart when you get to the campus that's right for you.

You manage your time. You design your Personal Study Schedule during the first two weeks of the semester, calculating hours and putting subjects in order. You've examined your course outlines and reviewed all the course materials so you know what you need to do each week. You follow your schedule, you study every course every day, and you put in all your hours. You keep copies of your Personal Study Schedule in the side pockets of your notebooks — and one on the fridge to remind your family when you're not available.

You understand that your schedule is your best defense against procrastination. *Procrastination kills (especially students)!* It's a good motto. You have a sign with this motto on the bulletin board in your room. You write it on the covers of your notebooks.

You're organized. You keep course outlines, and copies of your Personal Study Schedule and **Grade Tracker** in the pockets of your notebooks. These are the tools you use to manage each course. Because you review these pages regularly, you know what your teachers will cover each day, when tests are scheduled, when assignments are due, where you stand in each course, and that you have built the time to study into your days.

You're productive. At home, you have a well-equipped, quiet place to study, and everyone knows you shouldn't be interrupted during your scheduled study hours. Naturally, you don't take phone calls while you're studying, and you use your computer *only* for school work during study time. You stay as far away from distractions as possible.

You check on progress. At the end of every day, you make sure your homework assignments are done and you have studied all your courses thoroughly. You stay caught up and ahead of your course schedules. You record all your grades in your **Grade Tracker**.

You understand your opportunities. For you, school is invigorating. It gives you the chance to learn something NEW each day. You can see the big picture, and you've started making connections between courses. You view your education as a challenge, much like a competitive sport or playing a musical instrument. You're determined to play at a professional level — and win!

True, school has a strong social side to it, but it is not *only* a social place. It is your job. That means you respect your teachers, even the unpopular ones, and you respect your courses, even when they aren't your favorites ones. You're open-minded enough to go to school each day saying to yourself, *"All this is important for me, even in ways I don't yet understand."*

Being college smart is an attitude. You *value* your education for what it can do for you — in college and throughout your life. It is a privilege given to you so you can build your future.

You're ready. And as you go to your first class of the day, you've done the reading or solved the problems, or memorized the vocabulary that prepares you for this class and all of your classes. You've carefully done your homework because you know that your work signals your intellectual growth. You feel the same way about tests.

Ten minutes before class ends, the teacher says very casually, *"How about a quiz?"* No worries. You're ready.

You're involved. Class begins and you have your notebook in front of you. You learned a long time ago that notebooks are as important as textbooks, so you take good notes. You also know that keeping a complete notebook for each course is fundamental to your success. Your note-taking helps both your writing and thinking skills.

As you leaf through your notebook pages, your rough class notes are followed by rewritten notes, followed by outlines of textbook chapters. You've arranged important items that need to be memorized in different kinds of charts and lists (along with memory notes to help you fix them in your mind).

You've found a good place to sit in class: somewhere in the middle of the second row. You try to stay away from your friends who tend to talk too much.

You contribute. You've discovered that when students come to class prepared, listen, and participate, the class is livelier, more enjoyable, and you learn more. Because you've kept up with your reading and notes, you are always ready to join the discussion. You find you like being involved, contributing your thoughts, hearing what other students have to say, and getting your teacher's reaction. It's an energizing way to learn.

You're connected. You've got a good working relationship with your teachers because you've made it a point to talk to them. You know that if a course becomes difficult, they are going to help you in or out of the classroom. You can always go to them about study advice, too. As you are packing up to leave class, you ask your teacher a question you've been thinking about. The teacher tells you to stop by after school for a few minutes. No problem. You always discover interesting things when you talk with teachers. In fact, you appreciate the time teachers give you. You found out long ago that talking to teachers makes even the less-interesting classes (and teachers, for that matter) more thought-provoking. And isn't that what you want from every class? Mental excitement!

You're growing. As you walk to your next class and talk to your friends, you can actually feel that you've just energized your mind. It happens every time you are in a "learning mode." And perhaps the most important thing you are realizing about your mind: It grows as it processes knowledge, just as a tree processes sunlight, water, and nutrients. Long ago, you stopped thinking of your head as a container into which bits of information are dropped.

You know how to succeed. That's why you're a college smart student. Your great success didn't come naturally any more than playing a sport or an instrument. And you can't wait to get to college, because you'll know how to use all of the college smart Strategies to succeed. As a college student, with the skill and confidence of an expert learner, you know that you will discover the right career path.

When you're college smart, your life always looks and feels great! **RU READY?**

For parents — how you fit in

I've been a college adviser and teacher for 27 years — more than half my life — talking with countless students and parents. Yet it wasn't until my son got to high school that I really understood the conflicts and crises we parents experience in trying to help our kids get the best education possible. With every child, a new drama unfolds, sometimes moving so fast that we feel like we somehow fell asleep during the previous act. Or maybe we somehow missed the whole play. We'd like to say, *"Stop, I need to catch my breath. I need time to figure out what to do."* But there's no stopping life, any more than we can stop a play. *The show must go on,* and our children keep moving, from one educational stage to the next.

Even though I have the knowledge and strategies to handle any educational problem my son might face, I have still found myself occasionally, even frequently, on an emotional and intellectual roller coaster, trying to be both a good parent and a good educational counselor.

Conflicting roles

To my great frustration, I've discovered that being a parent and an academic guide can be contrary roles. Why? Well, by the time students get to high school, we parents have to begin fighting the urge to control. To a certain degree, we must stand back to let these emerging adults discover their own lives. Yet to succeed as educational guides (and parents), we know we cannot just let go. Nor should we.

These quasi-adults are not the same children we walked hand-in-hand to the bus stop in those early years of elementary school. And for us to let this new bus (high school or college life) take them away brings forth some pretty strong instincts. But we hold those feelings back, and off these young people go. As they grow up, the distance between us and them increases. The distance is necessary for a parent, but it's an impossible separation if you also want to be an effective educational guide. How do you do both?

To further complicate matters, our older children go from what we parents think of as just two roles — (1) son or daughter and (2) student — to a whole host of new roles: employee, athlete, boy/girlfriend, socialite, club president, student council member. We always knew these roles would come eventually, but suddenly, here they are, right there in front of us.

So there stands your son or daughter, who once looked like a drama of two or three actors, but now looks like the full cast of a Shakespearean play. My first reaction to this multiplication of life roles was to gasp and hope that I wouldn't suddenly be witnessing some great tragedy full of bad decisions, self-inflicted pain, betrayal, bad fate, and evil characters. Through my ups and downs, I fervently hoped my son would star in a life more like a lighthearted Broadway musical.

Learning to play your part

To help him, I had to find a script for myself — one that defined the dual role of parent and educational guide. So I merged my life as a parent with what I had learned from a lifetime of experience as a university academic administrator who developed advising programs. I created a set of guidelines for myself in my new role. These principles have helped me guide my son, and they should help you, too. While these guidelines won't guarantee a happy ending, they can create happy endings — or at the very least, create a smoother production as you move from act to act and scene to scene.

1. **Parents set the stage and direct the action.** A student cannot be compelled to learn. So parents, like teachers, should concentrate more on creating the best educational environment possible. Parents should talk regularly about the very practical value of learning. They should reward students for their efforts as much as for their successes. How much students study is as important as how many high grades they earn.

   The key is respect. If parents demonstrate respect for learning, avoiding negative comments about school and teachers, students will typically still respect learning, even when they occasionally lose the motivation to take it seriously.

2. **Your student's education is your education.** Until they leave the nest, most young people are too immature and lacking in self-discipline to be given full control over their educational lives. They still need you. Here's where the balancing act comes in. As a counselor/guide, you must be close to your student at the very time that the typical teen is pushing parents away to be more independent.

   But just as you control the behavior of teens in other areas of life — when and where they can go out, when they have to be home, etc. — you should also control their ordinary behavior as students. The 12 Strategies in this guidebook describe what that ordinary behavior should be. Even if you can direct them in only a few of the Strategies, some are better than none. The more, the better.

   The care, interest, and attention that parents gave to their students' learning when children were very young apply even more when children get older. However, the way you involve yourself may change. Don't let any significant gaps develop between you and your student. Keep saying to yourself, *"THEIR EDUCATION IS YOUR EDUCATION."* After all, you will most likely play a large role in its funding, and let's face it, it's a big bill. This guidebook will give you specific ways to help your older student on a daily basis.

3. **Reward your student's effort.** No matter how much we might all want our children to be honors students who achieve academic recognition, some students don't have the aptitude, the motivation, or the genuine interest in learning. What then?

   Think of it this way. Your student has *a job to do:* to take courses in school and earn the highest possible grades. Students, like employees, need supervision, encouragement, and a good working environment. You should provide these things. Reward your student not only for high grades, but also for effort: *regular hours of study and seriousness of purpose.* Some students will work hard in courses that are difficult for them and never earn an *A.*

We all want students to learn because *it's the right thing to do. It's their responsibility. It's important for their future. They will feel a sense of accomplishment.* However, abstract incentives will not work for all students. Abstractions will never motivate some students to work in courses they don't like. Arguing with these teens will not change their minds. If your student cannot be motivated to try harder by abstractions, you might consider rewards.

Weekly financial rewards are good motivators for students who are not otherwise motivated by grades and building a future that seems so far away. How many of us would go to work if we weren't paid for our efforts? Other students who won't respond to abstract incentives will respond to privileges that are attractive to them, like trading grades on tests for videogame or car privileges. Some adults may regard these as "crass" incentives. They might not be noble, but if they get the job done, that's better than not getting it done at all.

But even if you use incentives, like financial rewards or privileges, consistently reward your student with your sincere praise, encouragement, and appreciation. That's the best incentive there is.

The importance of parental encouragement aside for the moment, your efforts will be repaid very practically in the long run. Your student's academic success will ultimately reward you with many options for their educational advancement after high school. High grades and academic recognition translate into college scholarships and grants.

It's your guide, too.

This guidebook is meant as much for parents as for students. Its aim is to create College Smart Parents as well as College Smart Students, and I hope it helps you as much as it did me. It is not a book that is read once and put down. Student copies and parent copies should be well-thumbed, the result of using the book as an ongoing reference from semester to semester and year to year. Read through the Strategies. Visit the Web site **www.areyoureallyreadyforcollege.com** or **www.rureallyready4college.com.** Let the Strategies be your daily guide in helping both you and your student become college smart.

For teachers of orientation courses —
a very practical curriculum

Academic orientation courses that aim to give students a head start or a "leg up" in beginning a new phase of their education have been around for quite some time. I've strongly supported them at both the secondary-school and college level because students need "bridges" to help them get from one academic point to another. Orientation courses are one of those educational structures.

The changes from middle school to high school are significant, and for some students, really difficult to handle. All students need as much practical advice as possible to manage their new academic challenges. They also need advice about where their new educational experience is taking them: What happens *after* high school is a matter that every high school freshman should keep in mind. Most do not.

A practical perspective

I've written this book from the perspective of seeing the price that students pay for not looking beyond high school, for not maintaining a sense of what awaits them. It's a national tragedy that so few students enter college with the personal management skills to succeed.

The evidence is telling. Today's students graduate from high school with grade point averages that are the highest in 50 years, yet huge numbers drop out of college early, only one-third graduate in four years, and barely 60% graduate in under six years. The dropout rate at two-year colleges is 50% after the first year.

How many students go on to higher education? According to the Education Trust, 70% of high school graduates attend college within two years of graduation.

This guidebook is fundamentally different than any other book that's been published. For a quarter century, I have worked with literally thousands of students in trouble. My professional experience has given me a keen insight into the causes of their problems — problems rooted in the way students approach high school.

For *all* students

When I wrote **Are you *really* ready for college?**, I kept high school orientation courses in mind. This guidebook can be used as a textbook, providing a curriculum that details strategies for successful learning behavior. Or this guide can be assigned reading as a reference book that *all* students, even those not thinking about college, might use to make high school a better learning experience. Consider this statistic:

> **40% of high school graduates found that they were not prepared to meet the expectations that awaited them, whether they went to college or entered the workforce.**

The National Education Summit.

Organizing an approach to learning is *in itself* something to be learned. From the time today's high school students started kindergarten, they were told *what to learn* and to do their homework. The how-to-act-as-a-productive-learner both in and out of school was just supposed to develop on its own along the way. It never happened. Moreover, unaided, students are too immature to recognize that the skills they learn and develop in school are the same ones needed to become productive adults in the workplace! These skills in the Strategies are those that adults would bring to managing a project such as learning:

- setting specific goals.
- evaluating progress.
- gauging productivity.
- managing time.
- making use of resources.
- recognizing danger signals and adjusting.
- marking off milestones that signal accomplishments.

Learning how to learn

Students don't understand the initiative and effort needed to manage a college course load or the organization needed to handle their newfound independence. **Are you *really* ready for college?** fills the great void that professors recognize — the modern student's misunderstanding of what it means to be a student. The 12 Strategies focus on the "macro" issues, bringing what adults would term a project-management approach to learning. The Strategies show students how to self-sufficiently control their learning experiences, preparing prospective college students for the challenges that lie ahead.

This guide will help millions of college-bound students *use their high school years as a kind of dress rehearsal,* an opportunity to practice managing their courses *before* they get to college. Then, as college students, they will know how to control their course work AND get high grades AND graduate without wasting A LOT of time and money.

Non-college-bound students will learn skills that enable them to become lifelong learners. The Strategies will ready non-college-bound students to tackle whatever avenues they follow after graduation.

I hope that this book finds its way into orientation courses across the country.
If you are interested in building a course around this book, please go to
www.areyoureallyreadyforcollege.com or **www.rureallyready4college.com.**

For guidance counselors —
and others who give advice

As a guidance counselor in high school, you already know that the student population is increasing and will continue to increase for several years. A demographic bulge of students in high school and college is already with us, along with the pressure to give these millennium students more and better guidance.

If your school is typical, counselors, like many teachers, are already assigned more students than they can reasonably handle. The Strategies in this guide may help you work with students more efficiently.

You're a lifeline

As a person expected to give your students the best possible advice and counsel, you regularly try to do three things:

1. See that students stay on an academic track toward graduation.

2. Help students understand what's necessary during transitions: moving from middle school to high school, from one year to the next, and finally, from high school to college.

3. Help students set goals for today, for tomorrow, and for the rest of their lives.

I have been involved in the development and direction of college admissions and advising programs for many years. So I know very well the extraordinary job that guidance counselors do.

I especially know that your work is not always well-understood, much less appreciated. Parents, students, teachers, and even some administrators do not always realize how much counseling intersects with and supports classroom education.

Filling the educational gap

In some high schools, and many colleges, the philosophy of education is frequently rooted in these antique notions:

1. If students are going to class regularly, then they must be learning how to learn.

2. If students have busy lives, then they must know how to balance life and learning.

3. If students earn high grades, then they must understand the broad implications of learning on long-range success or failure.

One day in the life of a high school counselor would dispel many such misconceptions. Counselors, advisers, enlightened teachers, and school administrators know this axiom particularly applies to students as they advance in school:

**As students grow older, course content becomes more complex
and requires more individual initiative and personal responsibility.**

**Simultaneously, however, teachers become "specialists"
who teach subjects and whose schedules allow less time
to help students learn how to learn.**

Who fills the gap?

Typically, the gap is filled by counselors, advisers, learning-skills teachers, and a host of educational specialists. They fill the role of personal adviser for students — and it is a critical one.

When the personal growth of students is left unattended or unguided, students make serious mistakes. They blunder in selecting courses as they move from one year to the next, or they err in making good choices for themselves as they move from one level of education to the next. And worse, they lose track of why they are even in school.

As you well know, all students regularly need guidance and advice. At the very least, students need semesterly conversations with counselors about how their education fits amid confusing visions of their future and often distracting experiences in their daily lives. Some students need to learn how to get through a certain course. Other students need to learn to maintain or reach a level of academic self-sufficiency that will help them achieve their goals: graduation, college, and career.

Serving the whole student

Undoubtedly, a lot of good mentoring goes on between students and teachers. But the only person in charge of a student's *total welfare* is you, the counselor.

In my experience, I encountered the frustration of trying to deal with students' day-to-day issues. These issues often loomed large in their minds, distracting them as I was trying to help them focus on longer-term academic goals — which, to them, did not loom so large. For many students, the issues of immediate intellectual and personal development are being talked about less and less at home. In their need for privacy and independence, teenagers often withdraw from communicating with family. Because students would not bring their issues home, they brought them to my office. This may be your experience as well.

Advising strategies

Listening and talking with students across the desk is a great communication challenge. Early in my career, I had my own agenda, and I talked more than I listened. But then I learned that asking simple questions was far more effective:

1. *What three things are interfering with your academic success right now?*

2. *How and where do you see yourself at your next level of education?*

3. *List your courses for me and talk about each one.*

As students answered the questions, I listened more than I talked. I was giving the students the opportunity to set the agenda. Very quickly, I became much more effective.

And as I listened to them, I learned from them. Everything I know about student development, learning problems, and how their non-student lives interfere with their student lives, I learned from them.

This guidebook is a distillation of what thousands of high school and college students have told me and taught me. Therefore, this book is dedicated to all the students I have worked with over the years. But it is also dedicated to the academic counselors and advisers who work with determination to help students every day.

Review the 12 Strategies in this guidebook. They will give you a platform for helping students in a structured and concrete way that students can follow. I hope these Strategies will help you as they helped me. And furthermore, I hope your experience is the same as mine. Once you get young people to work on managing their lives on a *daily basis,* you can better help them manage their academic and personal lives on a *long-term basis.* You're in a pivotal position to help them understand themselves better and begin to shape a future they can truly call their own.

For high school teachers —
livelier discussions, more engaged students

How many perfect students have you had? I'm serious. Okay, then, if not perfect, how about really, really outstanding students? I've been in the front of many classrooms. Perhaps not as much as you, but I remember every one of the great experiences I've had with some truly excellent students over the years.

I think we can both agree that while "perfect" is not the adjective to use because that takes the humanity and reality out of the wonderfully human and real teaching experiences you have, one thing is certain: Great students are memorable. And they are memorable not just for their individual and personal accomplishments, but for two other very important reasons:

First, these students enliven classes; their very presence makes other students more interested in course material and more active in daily classroom activities. These students are extraordinary teaching devices and remarkable intellectual catalysts.

Second, they give you, as a teacher, a perfect tool to measure your pedagogical efforts. "Perfect" students test your teaching skills. When you see that they are satisfied, you know you have done your job, very well.

But have you had classes without these great students? We all have. Perhaps too many. But then, just when you begin to wonder if you have any teaching ability at all — because a certain class doesn't respond to your ultimate efforts — later in the day, you teach the same subject to a class that literally sparkles with intellectual enthusiasm. Why? Because of those particular students who respond and make you efforts worthwhile.

Unfortunately, my experience tells me that while the number of exceptional students entering college these days is as strong as ever, the number of students who have the potential *but not the discipline* for college is increasing dramatically. The statistics are evidence. 25% of college freshman do not return to the college where they started. And a little more than 33% of college students graduate in four years. The statistics are far worse for students at two-year colleges.

Discouraged by what I have seen among college students in recent years, I wrote this book in the hope that I could bring students back to some sense of traditional and normal pre-college education.

What's happening in high school classrooms is, I think, as good as ever. SATs and ACTs haven't changed that much over the years. But it's outside those classrooms that many students are failing. They are studying fewer hours than pre-college students have ever studied, and their understanding of learning as well as the effort and skill that real learning requires is unrealistic.

By that, I mean far too many students conceive of learning as an event rather than a process. When you, as a teacher, present the material to them in class, they expect to completely grasp it in an instant. If they don't, then something is wrong with your teaching, or something is wrong with them — they don't have the "genes" for math or the instinct for language. Effort, work, discipline? *"That's for athletes, isn't it?"*

My book tries to bring students back to basics, and in the process, I hope that the return to fundamentals that I promote will help you maintain that level of excitement and discovery that you would like to see in all your students and all your classes.

Good luck to you. I'll be thinking of you.

For principals —
consistency, performance, accountability

As an educational executive, your responsibilities have always been many, various, and challenging. These days, everything that already rests on your shoulders is given additional weight by that biggest responsibility of all – accountability. Everyone from parents to superintendents, to mayors, governors, and legislators looks to you for evidence, not only of increased success among your teachers and students, but also evidence of constant improvement in SATs and ACTs, Advanced Placement exams, and the college admission of your graduates.

My own experience as a college dean and professor for more than 25 years makes me appreciate more than ever the work that high school administrators do. As I wrote my book, **Are you *really* ready for college?**, high school officials were always on my mind.

I think that my book can help your school in many ways, particularly in the area of studying and learning.

It is written precisely for high schools students. It tells them that their success as a student is essential to their success not just for today, but for the future. And since most students continue their education beyond high school, they must seriously consider the effect of their high school efforts and their success on their post-graduate endeavors, whatever they may be.

In writing my book I also had in mind the many high school orientation courses that are required of freshmen. For whatever kind of course your school may offer, **Are you *really* ready for college?** would be a great textbook. It's a handbook that all your students can constantly learn from as they carry it with them throughout their high school careers.

When you order this book for your school, you receive a special discount at considerable savings. So please give consideration to **Are you *really* ready for college?** It may be just the book that your students and teachers need. To learn more, **www.areyoureallyreadyforcollege.com** or **www.rureallyready4college.com.**

LaVergne, TN USA
08 September 2010

196260LV00003B/50/P